Welcome to
Britain

Großbritannien
zum Lernen, Entdecken und Erleben

Oliver Astley

compact

Bisher sind in dieser Reihe erschienen:

- Benvenuti in Italia
- Bienvenido a España
- Bienvenue en France
- Welcome to Britain

Baierbrunner Str. 27, 81379 München
Ausgabe 2017
2. Auflage

Redaktion: Helga Aichele
Fachkorrektur: Nathalie Russell
Produktion: Ute Hausleiter
Titelabbildungen: shutterstock: Alhovik, Robert Biedermann, Debu55y,
jaroslava V, Martin Lisner, ronfromyork
Gestaltung: textum GmbH, München
Umschlaggestaltung: seitenwind GmbH, Design und Kommunikation, Regensburg

ISBN 978-3-8174-9666-2
381749666/2

www.compactverlag.de

Vorwort

Entdecken Sie Großbritannien mit all seinen Besonderheiten und erweitern Sie dabei ganz mühelos Ihre Sprachkenntnisse! *Welcome to Britain* ist Erlebnisreise und Sprachtraining in einem. Ein Streifzug durch verschiedene Regionen macht Lust, auch die vielfältigen Lebensgewohnheiten der Briten näher kennenzulernen, sich ihren Kulturschätzen zuzuwenden sowie ein Stück Geschichte zu ergründen.

Die 20 Kapitel entsprechen den Schwierigkeitsgraden A2 bis B2 und kommen daher geübten Anfängern und Fortgeschrittenen gleichermaßen entgegen. Je nach Kenntnisstand können Sie ein eher anspruchsvolleres Kapitel wählen oder sich beim Lesen eines leichteren Textes zurücklehnen. So lernen Sie mit Erfolg und verbessern nach und nach spürbar Ihr Englisch. Unbekannte Vokabeln können Sie jederzeit in den Vokabelkästen und am Ende des Buches nachlesen. Die eingestreuten Infokästen bieten zusätzlich allerlei Erstaunliches zu den verschiedenen Themen. Und anhand der Übungen nach jedem Kapitel können Sie Ihren Wissensstand und Ihre Sprachkenntnisse noch einmal überprüfen und festigen. Im Kapitel *Eating British* können Sie sich außerdem einige landestypische Rezepte herunterladen – natürlich auf Englisch. Scannen Sie einfach den QR-Code auf Seite 44 mit Smartphone oder Tablet!

Also, *Welcome to Britain* –
und viel Spaß beim Lesen und Lernen!

Contents

Great Britain and its regions

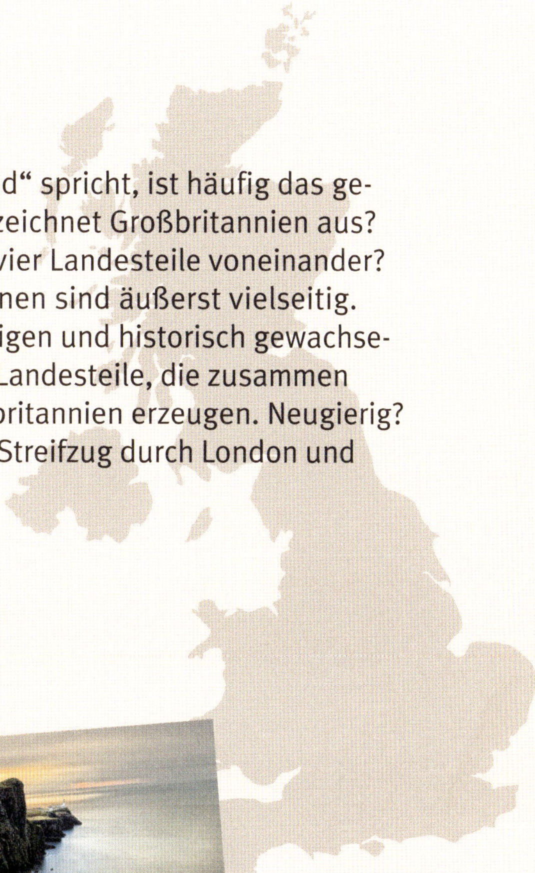

Wenn man leichthin von „England“ spricht, ist häufig das gesamte Land gemeint. Doch was zeichnet Großbritannien aus? Und wie unterscheiden sich die vier Landesteile voneinander? Großbritannien und seine Regionen sind äußerst vielseitig. Und es sind vor allem die vielfältigen und historisch gewachsenen Eigentümlichkeiten der vier Landesteile, die zusammen ein authentisches Bild von Großbritannien erzeugen. Neugierig? Dann kommen Sie mit auf einen Streifzug durch London und die Regionen!

Welcome to Britain!

One country, four nations

Britain? In fact we should say, "Welcome to the **United** Kingdom of Great Britain and Northern Ireland!" – but this is a very long name. So many people say "the United Kingdom", "Great Britain" or just "Britain" to describe the whole country.

You probably know that the United Kingdom **is made up of** England, Wales, Scotland and Northern Ireland. These four nations have a **common** history, political system and culture, but there are also many important differences. England is the biggest country with a much larger **population**, and London, the capital, is much larger than any other city in the UK. As a result, many things that you think are typically British are really icons of the capital: Big Ben, red buses, black taxi cabs and so on.

Geography and environment

With more than 6,000 islands, the British Isles are the seventh largest group of islands in the world. Only about 150 of these are **inhabited**. Great Britain, the largest, is made up of England, Wales and Scotland. Ireland, the second largest, has two parts: the Republic of Ireland and Northern Ireland.

Isle of Skye, Scotland

The total land area is around 250,000 km², which is about two-thirds the size of Germany. Britain is famous for its green hills and forests. There are also a few mountains, although none are as high as the Alps. The highest is Ben Nevis (1,344 m) in the Scottish Highlands. The largest mountain in Wales is Mount Snowdon (1,030 m).

An **impressive** coastline runs around the United Kingdom. From the beautiful White Cliffs of Dover to the dramatic Giant's Causeway in Northern Ireland, the coast is popular for **day trips** and holidays. And wherever you are in the UK, the sea is never more than 113 kilometres away! There are also 15 national parks in Britain, mainly in Scotland, Wales, northern England and around the southern coast.

Rain is a typical **feature** of British weather. However, it doesn't actually rain as much as people think. Did you know, for example, that more rain falls in Rome or Bordeaux than in London? Winter temperatures are also usually mild thanks to the **Gulf Stream**, so it doesn't snow very often.

The Union Jack

The national flag of the UK is called the Union Jack. It combines the flags of three **patron saints**: in addition to the red crosses of Saint George (England) and Saint Patrick (Ireland), it shows the white cross of Saint Andrew (Scotland) on a blue background. There is no Welsh **dragon** because Wales was already united with England when the first version of the Union Jack **appeared** in 1606. Today, it is an extremely popular design for souvenirs, clothes and accessories.

united	vereinigt, vereint	**day trip**	Tagesausflug
to be made up of	bestehen aus	**feature**	Merkmal
common	*hier:* gemeinsam	**Gulf Stream**	Golfstrom
population	Bevölkerung	**patron saint**	Schutzheilige(r)
inhabited	bewohnt	**dragon**	Drache
impressive	beeindruckend	**to appear**	erscheinen

1 Facts about Britain. Welche Antwort ist richtig? Kreuzen Sie an!

1. A typical British person drinks over a thousand cups of what each year?
   a) ❑ coffee
   b) ❑ tea
   c) ❑ whisky

2. What is the shortest distance between England and France?
   a) ❑ 33 km
   b) ❑ 66 km
   c) ❑ 99 km

3. How many of the British Isles are inhabited?
   a) ❑ about 6,000
   b) ❑ 4
   c) ❑ about 150

4. Which country is not represented on the Union Jack?
   a) ❑ Wales
   b) ❑ England
   c) ❑ Scotland

2 Great Britons. Unterstreichen Sie die sechs Schreibfehler in den folgenden Sätzen über berühmte Briten und korrigieren Sie sie! Die Namen sind fehlerfrei.

Sir Isaac Newton was born in the sevententh century. He was a brilliant mathematician who explained how Gravity works.

In Trafalgar Square their is a monument to Lord Nelson, an admiral who won a war against Napoleon.

Charles Darwin was a great english scientist who rote about evolution.

Most Brits say that Sir Winston Churchill is the most populer Brit of all time.

1. ....
2. ....
3. ....
4. ....
5. ....
6. ....

3 Crossword. Ergänzen Sie die Sätze über Großbritannien mit dem fehlenden Wort und lösen Sie das Rätsel!

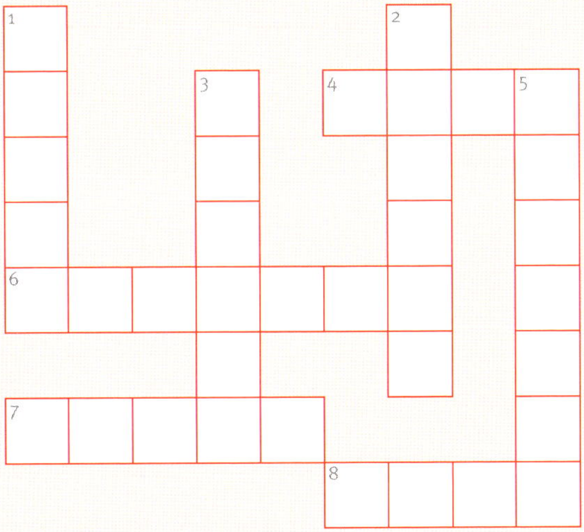

1. The currency *(Währung)* of the United Kingdom is the … .
2. The name of Prince William and Princess Catherine's first son is … .
3. A lot of Brits weigh themselves in … and pounds instead of kilograms.
4. People in Britain drive on the … side of the road.
5. … is a traditional light meal in the afternoon, usually with cake.
6. The Prime Minister lives on a road called … Street.
7. When someone sneezes, you usually say, "… you!"
8. The unit of distance on road signs is the …, not the kilometre.

4 Unscramble. Sortieren Sie die Buchstaben richtig!

1. This city has more canals than Venice.

   m m r i b a n i g h ....

2. This is the longest river in Britain.

   v r e n e s ....

3. This river runs through Oxford and London.

   s a t e m h ....

A nation, not a city

Not only is London the capital of the United Kingdom, it is also the largest metropolis in the European Union, with around 8.5 million **inhabitants**. And it is one of the most multicultural cities in the world: more than a third of Londoners were born in another country, and you can hear more than 300 different languages on the streets. This is just one reason why there is a **unique** atmosphere and feel to London. Indeed, many Brits see it as a world of its own within the UK.

London also has a fascinating history that goes back more than 2,000 years. Two great fires, **plague** and **attacks** could not stop its constant **growth**. For about four centuries, London was the centre of the British Empire, and today it is one of the world's most important cultural and **economic centres**.

Visitors to London will find lots of **attractions**. Some of the most famous **landmarks** are Tower Bridge, Piccadilly Circus, Westminster Abbey, Big Ben and Buckingham Palace. There are also world-class museums – many of them free – like the British Museum, the National Gallery or Madame Tussauds, the famous wax museum. Or why not go and see a **play** or a musical in "Theatreland" in the West End? There really is something for everyone. You can travel around on a red double-decker bus or enjoy a ride on the Tube – the world's oldest underground network.

London's skyline

London's skyline combines modern and traditional architecture like nowhere else in the country. St Paul's Cathedral sits on Ludgate Hill, the highest part of the city. The **Shard** is the tallest building in the EU, and from its 72nd floor you can enjoy an excellent view over the capital. Alternatively, the London Eye is Europe's tallest **observation wheel** with 32 capsules – one for each **borough** of the city. Other modern landmarks include an office tower known as "The **Gherkin**" and the bank towers of Canary Wharf.

London 2012

In summer 2012, London became the first city to **host** the modern Olympic Games three times. "London 2012" was an extremely successful event for Britain. In the **medal count**, Britain finished third after the United States and China.

The Tower of London

The Tower of London became a **World Heritage Site** in 1988 and is one of the most visited tourist attractions in Britain. The **fortress** was built in the eleventh century. English monarchs later used it not only as a palace, but also as a prison, a royal zoo, a **mint** and an archive. Visitors today can learn about the dark and bloody history of the Tower and take a look at the **Crown Jewels**. You can also see the famous **Yeomen Warders** in their colourful uniforms and the **ravens** that live there. A legend says that if the ravens ever leave, the Tower will fall... and the kingdom with it!

inhabitant	Einwohner(in)
unique	einzigartig
plague	Pest
attack	Angriff, Überfall
growth	Wachstum
economic centre	Wirtschaftszentrum
attraction	*hier:* Sehenswürdigkeit
landmark	Wahrzeichen
play	*hier:* Theaterstück
shard	Scherbe
observation wheel	Riesenrad
borough	Stadtbezirk
gherkin	Gewürzgurke
to host	ausrichten, Gastgeber sein
medal count	Medaillenspiegel
World Heritage Site	Welterbestätte
fortress	Festung
mint	Münzanstalt
Crown Jewels *pl*	Kronjuwelen
Yeomen Warders *pl*	königliche Leibgardisten
raven	Rabe

1 Speakers' Corner. Ergänzen Sie den Text mit den fehlenden Wörtern!

take **talk** **turn** **spoken** **say** **enjoy**

Every day of the week, you can 1. .... free entertainment at Speakers' Corner, next to Marble Arch in Hyde Park. You can even 2. .... part! Speakers' Corner has existed since the mid-1800s, and many different people go there to 3. .... to the public about political or religious subjects. Those who have 4. .... include famous names like Karl Marx and Winston Churchill. But anyone can 5. .... up and 6. .... what they think, so long as they stay within the laws of free speech.

2 Translation quiz. Übersetzen Sie die Wörter ins Englische und enträtseln Sie das Lösungswort!

1. Geschichte ☐ _ _ _ _ _ _
2. Jahrhundert _ _ _ _ _ _ ☐
3. Dom _ _ _ _ _ ☐ _ _ _
4. Aussicht _ _ ☐ _
5. Palast ☐ _ _ _ _ _
6. Sehenswürdigkeit _ _ _ _ ☐ _ _ _ _ _
7. Wachstum _ ☐ _ _ _ _
8. Wahrzeichen _ _ _ _ _ _ _ ☐

Hidden word: _ _ _ _ _ _ _ _

3 You can never get bored of London. Testen Sie Ihr London-Wissen!

1. An exciting annual tennis event in South West London that the British rarely win.
   W _ _ _ _ _ _ _ _ _
2. Where does the Queen keep the Crown Jewels?
   The _ _ _ _ _ of _ _ _ _ _ _
3. What do Brits usually call the London Underground?
   _ _ _ _ _ _ _
4. This huge museum of history and culture houses more than seven million items.
   _ _ _ B _ _ _ _ _ _ _ _ _ _ _ _ m
5. What is another name for the central business district known as "the City"?
   _ _ _ S _ _ _ _ _ _ M _ _ _
6. Which writer said: "When a man is tired of London, he is tired of life"?
   S _ _ _ _ _ J _ _ _ _ _ _

4 Spot the mistake. Unterstreichen Sie die sechs Grammatikfehler im folgenden Textabschnitt und korrigieren Sie sie!

Not only is London the capital of the United Kingdom, it is also the largest metropolis in the European Union, with around 8.5 million inhabitants and 45 universities. It is also one of the multiculturalest cities in the world: more than a third of Londoners are born in another country and less than half is white British. If you walk through the streets of London, you are hearing more than 300 different languages, and it gives thousands of restaurants where you can try food from every country on the world.

1. .... 2. ....

3. .... 4. ....

5. .... 6. ....

From countries to counties

The United Kingdom is **divided up** into **counties**. There are 48 in England alone, and the differences from region to region are greater here than in the other three nations. Many counties are named after their largest city, such as Oxford in Oxfordshire. The word "shire" is an old word for "county", and for many people both words are synonymous with green countryside and tradition. J. R. R. Tolkien also called the home of the hobbits "the Shire". Each county has its own regional and sometimes very strong identity as well as a **distinctive** accent.

Capital: London

Population: 53.9 million

Patron saint: St George

National flower: rose

Town and country life

The UK was the world's first industrialized country. In the nineteenth century, more and more people moved away from the countryside to find work in cities like London or Manchester. Today, nine out of ten Brits live in towns and cities. The **vast majority** of jobs, schools and homes are in urban areas. As a result, many people live in a small **space**, especially in England. But cities also have a lot to offer: Liverpool, for example, is one of the most interesting cities in the world. It has many galleries and combines a rich **cultural heritage** with an exciting, modern image.

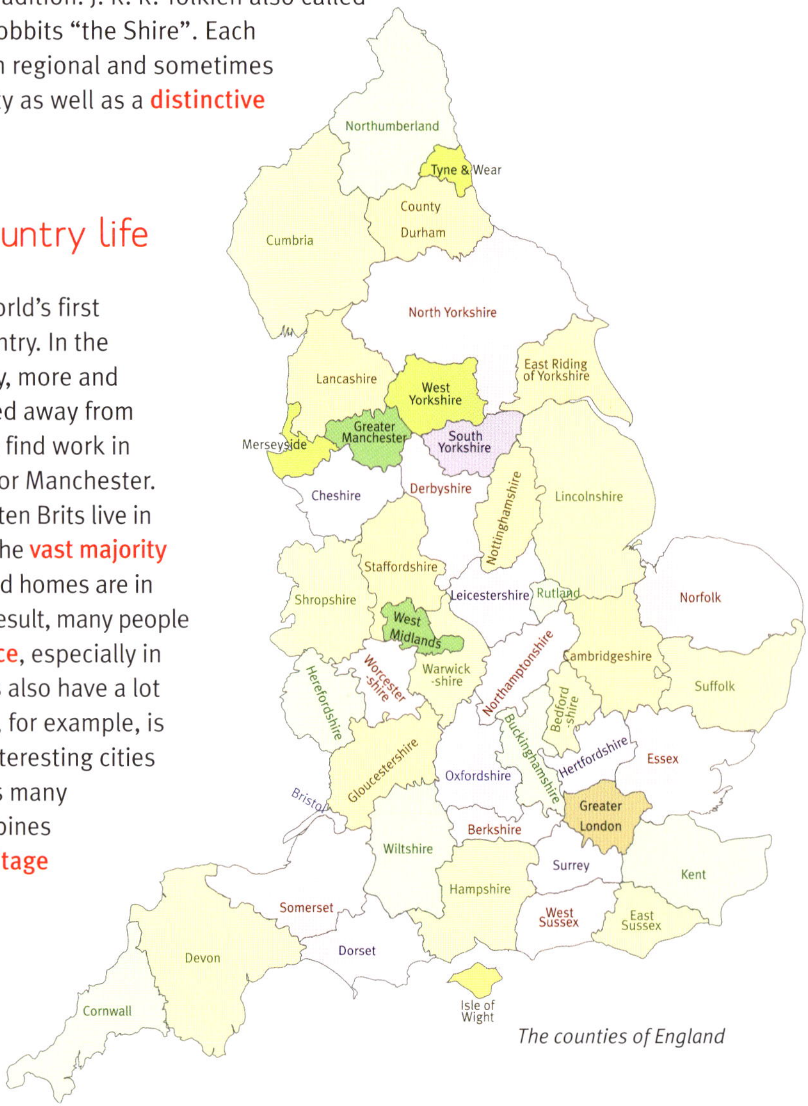

The counties of England

In smaller cities you will find lots of historic buildings and famous **landmarks**: great universities in Oxford and Cambridge, spectacular cathedrals in York, Winchester and Ely, **ancient** castles in Warwick and Bamburgh, and so on. And it is still possible to find an echo of "**Merry England**" in small country towns. Look out for one of the festivals or county **fairs** that celebrate the **rural** way of life!

North and south

The **north–south divide** describes the social, **economic** and political differences between the south of England and the rest of the United Kingdom. Power and investment are concentrated in the South, while **mining** and industry were once mostly in the North. Today, the divide seems to be bigger than ever before: London and the South East are becoming richer and richer, while many other parts of the country are in stagnation.

An idyllic landscape in Yorkshire

People often say "it's **grim** up north", but the situation is more complex. The cost of living is not as high here as in and around London. There are also wonderful countryside areas in the North, including the spectacular Lake District and the wild North York Moors. Most people also say that northerners are more open and friendly. Why not go and find out for yourself?

The mild South West ("the West Country") is another charming part of England with lots of seaside towns and beautiful national parks. It is warmer in this part of the country, and there are even **palm trees** in Cornwall and Devon.

divided up	aufgeteilt in
county	Grafschaft
distinctive	charakteristisch
vast majority	überwältigende Mehrheit
space	Raum
cultural heritage	Kulturerbe
landmark	Wahrzeichen
ancient	antik, uralt
Merry England	gutes altes England
fair	Ausstellung, Jahrmarkt
rural	ländlich
north–south divide	Nord-Süd-Gefälle
economic	wirtschaftlich
mining	Bergbau
grim	*hier*: hart, trostlos
palm tree	Palme

1 In the countryside. Bringen Sie die Buchstaben in die richtige Reihenfolge und ordnen Sie die Übersetzungen richtig zu!

1. ☐ t a r e m s .... a) Steinmauer
2. ☐ t o m u n i n a .... b) Wald
3. ☐ s o t e n l a l w .... c) Berg
4. ☐ d e g e h .... d) Acker
5. ☐ t r e f o s .... e) Fluss
6. ☐ f d e l i .... f) Bach
7. ☐ v r i e r .... g) Hecke

2 Verb forms. Bringen Sie die Verben in die richtige Verbform!

Napoleon once 1. say .... that England is a "nation of shopkeepers". In British city centres today you will find many of the same shops you find in cities all over Europe, but some are different. There 2. be .... a lot of charity shops, such as Oxfam and the British Red Cross, that 3. sell .... second-hand clothes, books and things for the house. Friendly locals often work there in their free time. Away from the high street, where people actually 4. live ...., the much-loved corner shop still 5. exist .... These shops are often owned by Pakistanis or Indians, especially in cities, and they are open from very early to very late. They seem to sell everything, from milk, tobacco and tinned soup to toothpaste and dog food! The Brits couldn't 6. survive .... without their corner shops!

3 Vocabulary. Welches Wort ist das „schwarze Schaf"? Unterstreichen Sie das Wort, das nicht in die Reihe passt!

1. **region city area county**
2. **grim historic famous spectacular**
3. **heritage tradition history mining**
4. **North rich Manchester industry**

4 Facts about England. Bringen Sie die Wörter in die richtige Reihenfolge!

1. **an Wide invented World the Englishman Web**

   ....

2. **official 300 the England was French language for in years**

   ....

3. **stamp appeared the in in world's 1840 first England**

   ....

4. **is England's one biggest of exports beef**

   ....

5 Nicknames. Welchen Spitznamen haben die Leute aus folgenden Städten in England? Ordnen Sie zu!

1. ☐ London	a) Brummie
2. ☐ Manchester	b) Scouser
3. ☐ Birmingham	c) Ciderhead
4. ☐ York	d) Mancunian
5. ☐ Newcastle	e) Cockney
6. ☐ Liverpool	f) Geordie
7. ☐ Bristol	g) Tyke

A famous Scouser: Sir Simon Rattle

Druids and dragons

According to stories from long ago, Wales was once home to Druids and Celtic poets known as bards. These Celts were in fact the Britons who lived all over the island before Roman and Saxon **invaders** pushed them to the west. The legendary King Arthur is their most famous leader, and the red dragon as a symbol for Wales goes back to a story about him.

Capital: Cardiff

Population: 3.1 million

Patron Saint: St David

National flower: daffodil

Sheep and castles

There are a lot of high hills and deep valleys in Wales, and the ground in many areas is poor for growing vegetables. However, it is perfect for sheep! In fact, there are about three sheep for every person in Wales. The green hills are also home to more than 600 castles – more per **square kilometre** than any other country in the world.

The Welsh word for Wales is "Cymru" [ˈkʌmri], which means "land of fellow countrymen". The original meaning of the English word "Welsh" is "foreign" or "not Anglo-Saxon". These are two very different definitions for the same nation!

Cardiff

Wales is a peaceful and green country. Only three of its cities have a population of more than 100,000 people, and all of these are on the south coast. Cardiff, the capital, is easy to visit on foot. Highlights for visitors include the National Museum, Cardiff Castle, Cardiff Bay and the extraordinary Millennium Stadium, which opened in 1999. Cardiff is also home to the Senedd, which houses the **National Assembly** of Wales. It was created after the people of Wales decided in 1997 that they wanted their own government for certain **issues**.

A bilingual culture

There are two official languages in Wales: English and Welsh, a Celtic language. Everybody speaks English and around half a million people **are fluent in** Welsh. All children have to learn Welsh at school until they are 16, and there are TV and radio programmes in Welsh. Road signs and place names are in both languages, though trying to pronounce them will certainly be a **challenge** for most visitors! For example, could you ask for a ticket to this railway station, which has the longest name in the world?

A creative nation

Music and poetry have a special place in Welsh culture. In addition to world-famous singers of pop and classical music, such as Sir Tom Jones and Bryn Terfel, Wales is famous for its **male voice choirs**. The eisteddfod [aɪˈsteðvɒd] is a popular type of festival that celebrates Welsh poetry, music and dance.

invader	Eindringling	**national assembly**	Nationalversammlung
daffodil	Narzisse	**issue**	Thema
square kilometre	Quadratkilometer	**to be fluent in ...**	... fließend sprechen
fellow countrymen *pl*	Landsleute	**challenge**	Herausforderung
		male voice choir	Männerchor

1 Facts about Wales. Welche Antwort ist richtig? Kreuzen Sie an!

1. St David's in South Wales is the world's smallest cathedral city. Roughly how many people live there?
   a) ❑ 1,600 b) ❑ 6,600 c) ❑ 11,600

2. The first company in Britain to brew lager was in Wrexham, North Wales. It was opened in 1881 by immigrants from which country?
   a) ❑ Germany b) ❑ Austria c) ❑ Switzerland

3. Which of these is named after a famous Welsh geographer?
   a) ❑ The Gobi Desert b) ❑ Niagara Falls c) ❑ Mount Everest

4. Hay-on-Wye is a small town on the Welsh border with a population of 1,300, but it has more than 50 shops. It is the world's largest market for...?
   a) ❑ wool clothes b) ❑ used books c) ❑ war memorabilia

St David's Cathedral

Millennium Centre, Cardiff

2 Adverb or adjective? Unterstreichen Sie die richtige Variante!

1. Sheep follow each other **blind** / **blindly**.
2. It is **possible** / **possibly** that King Arthur was a real person.
3. Dragons can fly very **good** / **well**.
4. About one in six Welsh people can speak **fluent** / **fluently** Welsh.
5. The Welsh are **famous** / **famously** good at singing.

3 Crossword. Vervollständigen Sie das Kreuzworträtsel mit den fehlenden Präpositionen.

1. You will see bilingual signs when you go ... the border into Wales.
2. Some sheep are standing ... the castle and the sea.
3. The dragon flew ... the mountain and disappeared out of sight.
4. Two children were standing ... to each other on stage.
5. After the party, they stayed up singing all ... the night.
6. Marion hasn't been to Cardiff for ... ten years.
7. I looked ... from the hotel window and saw Tom Jones!

4 True or false? Welche Aussagen sind korrekt? Kreuzen Sie an!

1. There used to be Celts throughout England as well as in Wales. ☐
2. The Welsh flag was not official until 1959. ☐
3. Cardiff is a small city and most of it is inside an old, large castle. ☐
4. Some children in Wales choose not to learn Welsh. ☐
5. You don't have to be from Wales to enjoy an eisteddfod. ☐
6. Most people in Wales live on the north coast. ☐

A Celtic homeland

Capital: Edinburgh

Population: 5.3 million

Patron saint: St Andrew

National flower: **thistle**

Just like the Welsh and the Irish, the Scots are a Celtic nation. The Scots never made it easy for potential **invaders** like the Romans or the English – as fans of the film *Braveheart* will know. And a strong Scottish identity grew out of the conflict between Scotland and England, which lasted for centuries. Some aspects of Celtic culture began to disappear after 1746, when the Scots were **defeated** at Culloden and new laws stopped them from carrying **swords** or wearing **kilts**. However, all things Scottish became fashionable in the 1850s when Queen Victoria bought Balmoral Castle, near Aberdeen. The Queen still likes to spend her summer holidays here together with her family.

Theatre poster, ca 1900

Lochs and monsters

The landscape north of the English border is extremely **diverse**, with rolling hills in the Lowlands and wild mountain landscapes in the Highlands. Just as spectacular are the 30,000 **freshwater lakes** known as lochs: Loch Lomond is the largest (71 km^2) and Loch Morar the deepest (310 m), but the most famous is, of course, Loch Ness. Not only does this loch contain more water than all the lakes in England and Wales together, it is also home to Nessie, the legendary (or is it?) Loch Ness monster!

Glasgow and Edinburgh

Glasgow is the largest city in Scotland, but it is not the capital. Culturally, it has a lot to offer, including art galleries, a great alternative scene and some of the wildest pubs and clubs in Britain. The capital, Edinburgh, is built around a majestic castle. The Edinburgh International Festival, the largest arts festival in the world, celebrates theatre, art, dance and music for three weeks every summer. It also offers a famous alternative scene: visitors to the Fringe, as it is called, can enjoy international comedy at its best. And don't forget **Hogmanay** – one of the world's biggest New Year's Eve parties.

A view over Edinburgh

Tradition meets modernity

Scotland is known all over the world for **bagpipes**, men in kilts, **haggis** and whisky. These traditional national symbols go hand in hand with the Highland Games – a celebration of Celtic music, dance and sport. But ask a Scotsman what defines his country, and he will probably talk about the landscape, a long tradition of music and the arts, and the people. Today, like Wales, Scotland has its own regional government. However, Scottish **independence** is still a debated **issue**: a referendum in September 2014 showed that only 55.3% of Scots were against independence.

bonnie *Scottish*	hübsch, schön
invader	Eindringling
thistle	Distel
to defeat	besiegen, schlagen
sword	Schwert
kilt	Schottenrock
diverse	vielfältig
freshwater lake	Süßwassersee
Hogmanay *Scottish*	Silvester
bagpipes *pl*	Dudelsack
haggis	Gericht aus Schafsinnereien
independence	Unabhängigkeit
issue	Thema

1 Passives. Wandeln Sie die Sätze zum Hadrianswall ins Passiv um!

1. The Romans built Hadrian's Wall to protect themselves from the "barbarians" in the north.

   ....

2. You can follow the popular Hadrian's Wall footpath for 135 km.

   ....

3. The path will take you through some beautiful, wild and remote countryside.

   ....

4. UNESCO made Hadrian's Wall a World Heritage Site in 1987.

   ....

2 Great Scots. Wer hätte das gesagt? Ordnen Sie zu!

a) Robert Burns b) James Watt c) John Dunlop
d) Alexander Graham Bell e) John Logie Baird

1. ☐ "I invented the first working television in 1924."
2. ☐ "I'm the national poet of Scotland. I lived in the late eighteenth century, but people still read my poems – especially at big parties in January with lots of food and drink."
3. ☐ "I invented the telephone, but I never had one in my own study. It's much better to work in silence without that thing ringing every twenty minutes!"
4. ☐ "I was a vet on the west coast of Scotland. I loved cycling, and I found a way to improve the tyres by using air instead of solid rubber.
5. ☐ "I improved the steam engine. In fact, you could say that I invented the modern steam engine. I also developed a way of measuring electrical power."

Did you know?
About 11% of Scottish people have red hair – more than anywhere else in the world!

3 Gretna Green. Lesen Sie den Absatz über Gretna Green und übersetzen Sie die fehlenden Begriffe ins Englische!

Gretna Green is a small 1. Dorf .... in the south of Scotland, just north of the 2. Grenze .... It is extremely 3. beliebt .... for 4. Hochzeiten .... among the Scottish and the English. Some 200 years ago, it was impossible to marry under the age of 21 in England without your parents' permission. Young lovers therefore left 5. Zuhause .... and got married here, where boys could marry at 14 and girls only had to be 12! There are now 1,500 weddings every year in Gretna Green, and for this 6. Grund .... it is always a busy place. 7. Heutzutage ...., everyone in Britain can get married at the age of 16, but they need parental consent until they are 18 – 8. außer .... the Scottish!

Most Scots spoke Gaelic before the eighteenth century. Today, only a few thousand people speak the old Celtic language, mostly on small islands in the north. Nevertheless, Scottish English ("Scots") has its own colourful vocabulary and grammar.

4 Scottish English. Wie sagt man das in Standard Englisch? Ordnen Sie zu!

1. ☐ tattie
2. ☐ bonnie
3. ☐ wee
4. ☐ bairn
5. ☐ kirk
6. ☐ lassie
7. ☐ Hogmanay
8. ☐ loch

a) child
b) girl
c) church
d) potato
e) small
f) pretty
g) lake
h) New Year's Eve

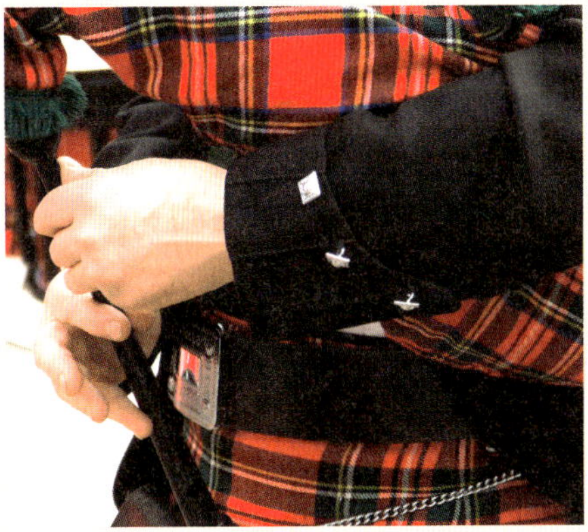

A Scottish piper

A little Irish magic

It is easy to get confused when talking about Ireland. Politically speaking, Ireland is divided into two parts: the independent Republic of Ireland in the south, and Northern Ireland, which is a part of the United Kingdom.

Division and conflict in Northern Ireland have dominated the headlines for decades, but the country has a long history that is just as varied as anywhere else in the UK. It also has a lot to offer in terms of natural beauty, and don't forget the legendary **hospitality** of the Irish that makes visitors feel so welcome!

Capital: Belfast

Population: 1.8 million

Patron saint: St Patrick

National flower: **shamrock**

Belfast

Belfast is sometimes called "the Old Smoke" because it used to be the only industrial town in Northern Ireland. It was an important shipbuilding city during the Victorian period, and its most famous export was the enormous **liner** *Titanic,* which sank in 1912. Most of the city's great buildings **date back to** the nineteenth century, such as Queen's University, the **splendid** City Hall and the Palm House in the Botanic Gardens.

A trip to the country

Of the six counties in Northern Ireland, County Antrim welcomes the most visitors. In addition to the capital city of Belfast, it offers peaceful sandy beaches and excellent golf courses. However, the most famous sight is the Giant's Causeway, a spectacular rock formation that is 60 million years old. According to legend, an Irish giant once built a path across the sea to Scotland, and these rocks are all that remain. Northern Ireland is also home to a more modern legend: most of the hit TV series *Game of Thrones* is filmed there.

Seeing past the Troubles

The violent conflict in Northern Ireland between 1968 and 1998 is known as the Troubles. Over three decades, more than 3,600 people lost their lives and thousands more were injured. It is important to understand that people were not fighting about religion, but about unequal **economic opportunities** and **civil rights**. However, religion also played a part in the conflict: the Catholic minority in the North are mostly Nationalists who want all of Ireland to be one country. The Protestant majority, on the other hand, are usually Unionists and want Northern Ireland to remain in the United Kingdom. This division has existed for centuries.

The situation has been peaceful since the **Good Friday** Agreement of 1998. Today, both Nationalists and Unionists are represented in Northern Ireland's parliament, but there are still **tensions**. For example, 34 kilometres of tall walls known as "peace lines" separate Catholics and Protestants in parts of Belfast and other towns.

Nationalist mural in a Catholic area

Unionist symbols in Belfast

shamrock	Kleeblatt
division	Spaltung, Trennung
hospitality	Gastfreundlichkeit
liner	Passagierschiff
to date back to	stammen aus
splendid	prächtig
economic opportunities *pl*	wirtschaftliche Möglichkeiten
civil rights *pl*	Bürgerrechte
Good Friday	Karfreitag
tensions *pl*	Spannungen
mural	Wandgemälde

1 Translation quiz. Übersetzen Sie die Wörter ins Englische und enträtseln Sie das Lösungswort!

1. Spannungen ___ [ ] _____
2. Schlagzeile [ ] ________
3. Riese __ [ ] __
4. wirtschaftlich ______ [ ] __
5. Minderheit ____ [ ] ___
6. Gastfreundlichkeit _ [ ] __________
7. Bürgerrechte [ ] ____ ________
8. Felsformation ___ [ ] _________

Hidden word: ________

> The Troubles really began back in the 1600s, when Protestants from Scotland and England were given land in Ireland. From then on, these people had better opportunities than the Catholics. In the city of Derry, an enormous wall was built to protect the settlers from the local population. It is the only completely walled city on the island today. Unionists still call it Londonderry, the name it was given by the settlers to symbolize English power.

2 Match up. Ordnen Sie die Begriffe der richtigen Definition zu!

1. [ ] Celtic tiger
2. [ ] Crown Liquor Saloon
3. [ ] Titanic Quarter
4. [ ] Antrim
5. [ ] Unionist
6. [ ] Nationalist

a) The most famous pub in Belfast
b) One of the six counties of Northern Ireland
c) Someone who wants Northern Ireland to belong to the Republic of Ireland
d) Someone who wants Northern Ireland to belong to the United Kingdom
e) A name for Ireland in the 1990s and later when its economy was growing fast
f) The renovated dockland area of Belfast

Typically British!

Was zeichnet die britische Lebensart aus – was ist „typisch britisch“? Laut Klischee trinken die Briten gerne Tee und bewundern die stoische Haltung der stets lächelnden Queen. Sie sind berühmt für ihren trockenen Humor, lieben kuriose Sportarten wie Cricket und pflegen selbst exzentrische Traditionen mit einem ironischen Augenzwinkern. Und auch kulinarisch hat das Land mehr zu bieten, als man denkt. Auf unserem Streifzug begegnen wir steifen Oberlippen, stehen geduldig Schlange und machen Station im Pub um die Ecke.

Alles *very British* eben!

A very famous family

For many people, the royal family represents tradition and stability. The Windsors give the British a sense of national identity and are famous all over the world. Many tourists from the United Kingdom and even **from abroad** travel to London for special events such as the **Diamond Jubilee** and hope to see the royal family on a **walkabout**. And in souvenir shops, you will find postcards, teacups and hundreds of other gifts showing the most popular royals. You can even buy paper masks of Diana and the **late** Queen Mother!

Queen Elizabeth II began her **reign** in February 1952, and she is the longest-lived monarch in British history. In September 2015, at the age of 89, she also became Britain's longest-reigning monarch – a record **previously** held by Queen Victoria, her great-great-grandmother. However, the media usually focus on the younger generations, especially Prince William and Princess Catherine, the **Duke** and **Duchess** of Cambridge. Around two billion people all over the world watched the marriage of Britain's future king in 2011.

The British monarchy

State Opening of Parliament

Officially, the British monarch is **Head of State** and **Supreme Governor** of the Church of England, also known as the Anglican Church. Once a week, the Queen discusses politics with the Prime Minister. However, she has no real political power. Instead, her role is ceremonial and symbolic. For example, she opens Parliament, signs new **laws**, welcomes important guests to Buckingham Palace and represents the nation. During the opening ceremony of the Olympic Games in 2012, the Queen **delighted** the world by appearing in a funny sketch with Daniel Craig's James Bond.

King George V, a cousin of Kaiser Wilhelm II, changed the name of the royal family in 1917 because of the political situation in Europe: the German House of Saxe-Coburg and Gotha became the very British-sounding House of Windsor. Windsor is a small town near London with a castle from the 11th century.

A British republic?

In general, the Brits love their royal family! About three-quarters of the population **support** the monarchy, and many people take a strong interest in the lives of the royals. Many of the royals **are actively involved in** British life, too. They support **the arts** and do a lot of work to **promote** international relations, **scientific research** and **charitable** organizations.

Some people argue that having a king or queen is not democratic. After all, the motto of the British monarch is *Dieu et mon droit*, which means "God and my right". The critics think that the idea that anyone has a **divine right** to rule over a country is both **old-fashioned** and totally irrelevant in the 21st century. Others believe that the royal family is simply too expensive, but in 2014 the cost to each **resident** of the United Kingdom was just 56 pence – about the same price as a chocolate bar.

from abroad	aus dem Ausland
Diamond Jubilee	60. Thronjubiläum
walkabout	*hier:* Bad in der Menge
late	*hier:* verstorben
reign	Regentschaft
previously	zuvor
duke, duchess	Herzog, Herzogin
Head of State	Staatsoberhaupt
Supreme Governor	*hier:* Kirchenoberhaupt
law	Gesetz
to delight	erfreuen, entzücken
to support	unterstützen
to be actively involved in	sich aktiv einbringen in, sich engagieren
the arts *pl*	*hier:* Kunst und Kultur
to promote	fördern
scientific research	wissenschaftliche Forschung
charitable	wohltätig, gemeinnützig
divine right	göttliches Recht
old-fashioned	altmodisch
resident	Einwohner(in)

1 True or false? Welche Aussagungen zum Königshaus sind korrekt? Kreuzen Sie an!

1. The Windsors have an English name but they are not British. ☐
2. One of the Queen's granddaughters has an Olympic medal. ☐
3. In private, Prince Philip sometimes calls the Queen "sausage". ☐
4. The Queen Mother was over 100 years old when she died. ☐
5. The monarchy is not very popular in the United Kingdom. ☐
6. Prince Harry once dressed up in Nazi uniform for a party. ☐
7. No king or queen has refused to sign a new law since 1707. ☐

2 Castles and palaces. Welche Residenzen sind abgebildet? Ordnen Sie zu!

☐ Buckingham Palace ☐ Sandringham House ☐ Windsor Castle
☐ The Palace of Holyroodhouse ☐ Balmoral Castle ☐ The Tower of London

1.

2.

3.

4.

5.

6.

3 Buckingham Palace. Unterstreichen Sie die richtige Variante!

1. The Palace covers 77,000 m^2; there **is** / **are** 775 rooms and 760 windows.
2. Queen Victoria became the first monarch to use the Palace as an official residence in 1837. The building was **still** / **already** over 200 years old when she moved in.
3. John Nash (1752–1835) was a British architect who **has redesigned** / **redesigned** the Palace and many other elegant buildings in London.
4. The Palace has **an own** / **its own** post office, swimming pool and cinema.
5. In the mid-nineteenth century, a teenager called Edward Jones broke into the Palace three times. He once even stole **one of** / **some of** Queen Victoria's underwear.

4 The Queen's Crossword. Lösen Sie das Kreuzworträtsel!

1. The Queen shook hands with the public and received flowers during her … .
2. A democratic state without a monarchy is a … .
3. The Queen is … (3 words) in the United Kingdom and 16 Commonwealth countries.
4. The Queen is popular not only in her own country, but also … .
5. Prince William is the … of Cambridge.
6. Queen Elizabeth II began her … at the age of 25.
7. The Queen celebrated her Diamond … in 2012 after 60 years on the throne.
8. The animal on the royal flag is the … – a symbol of bravery and strength.

Class and social status

A typical Brit?

When you think of a typical British person, do you imagine a man with a **bowler hat** or rowdy football fans? These **stereotypes** show that the class system is still **alive and kicking** in British **society**. The most obvious examples are the monarchy and the House of Lords, but both the working class and the middle class have a strong voice in Britain today. In many ways, the **class divide** still exists despite greater social mobility since the 1950s.

The middle class has grown enormously since the post-war era and now describes anyone who owns a nice house and has a stable job as well as a little money in the bank. There is also a new elite of very rich business tycoons and celebrities. In this sense, Britain has become more like America, where money and influence define social status more than birth and education. A good example is David Beckham, who began life as the son of a hairdresser and a **kitchen fitter**. He and his family are certainly not working class now! Individual success is therefore more important than class labels in modern society.

Despite social change, most Brits still tend to **judge** and label others according to their background, lifestyle and accent. This means that the way you speak and behave – from how you drink your tea to how you dress and which music you listen to – will tell people more about your class than how much money you have in the bank. The traditional view is that you can become rich, but you cannot become a gentleman.

What is class? In an important survey in 2013, more than 150,000 Brits were asked about how much money they earn, spend and save, to list the professions of their friends and family and to talk about their hobbies. The results found seven different social classes. Why not take the test yourself? Search online for "the Great British Class Survey".

If you speak without a regional accent and use **educated** language, people might call you "**posh**" – and this is not generally meant in a nice way! Speaking with a strong accent and using a lot of slang is usually a sign of a working class background. That said, you could be from any level of society these days, and many successful people are even proud of their regional accent or working class roots.

Snobbery and tolerance

Almost every language in Europe has adopted the English word "snob". It is therefore fair to say that snobbery is a very British characteristic! Of course, it is the result of basing social status on background and culture. Snobbery is the tendency to look down on others because of the job they have, how they dress, which supermarket they use or where they live, for example. But **inverted snobbery** – disliking people just because they are posh – is also extremely common. People might **tease** a relative or colleague about driving an **old banger** or eating fast food, but they would probably tease them more for owning an expensive new car made in Germany or drinking Earl Grey tea. "That's *so* middle class!" they might say – and this would not be a compliment! For them, speaking like a **chav** is probably better than speaking like a **toff**.

A stereotypical chav

Despite their snobbery, the British are actually a tolerant nation. The country that gave the world punk rock and the original eccentric allows teachers and police officers to dress in line with their religious beliefs, for example. In 2014, the UK also became one of the first countries in Europe to allow **same-sex marriage**.

bowler hat	Melone
stereotype	Klischee, Vorurteil
alive and kicking	höchst lebendig
society	Gesellschaft
class divide	Klassenunterschiede
kitchen fitter	Kücheneinrichter(in)
to judge	beurteilen
educated	gebildet
⚡ **posh**	*hier*: zur Oberschicht gehörend, „schnieke"
inverted snobbery	umgekehrter Snobismus
to tease	necken
⚡ **old banger**	Klapperkiste
⚡ **chav**	Proll
⚡ **toff**	feiner Pinkel
same-sex marriage	gleichgeschlechtliche Ehe

1 Mind your language! Für viele alltägliche Begriffe gibt es eine sogenannte „U“ (upper class) und eine „non-U“ (not upper-class) Variante, die man verwendet, um „posher“ zu klingen. Ordnen Sie zu!

U expression	non-U expression
1. ☐ napkin	a) perfume
2. ☐ jam	b) serviette
3. ☐ lavatory	c) dentures
4. ☐ sofa	d) toilet
5. ☐ scent	e) settee
6. ☐ false teeth	f) preserve

2 Famous Brits. Welche berühmten Briten werden beschrieben? Ordnen Sie zu!

a) This singer and musician from Newcastle upon Tyne is the son of a milkman.
b) This supermodel is the daughter of a Jamaican-born dancer and single mum.
c) This footballer and fashion icon is the son of a hairdresser and a kitchen fitter.
d) This politician and former British Prime Minister is the son of a London stockbroker and had an elite education at Eton and Oxford.
e) This actor is the grandson of a London mayor and was educated at Eton College.
f) This soul singer was raised in London and Brighton by a single mum who works as a furniture-maker.

1. ☐ Adele

2. ☐ Damian Lewis

3. ☐ David Cameron

4. ☐ Sting

5. ☐ Naomi Campbell

6. ☐ David Beckham

3 Passive. Schreiben Sie die folgenden Sätze in der entsprechenden Passivform um!

1. Almost every European language has adopted the word "snob".
   The word "snob" has been adopted by almost every European language.
2. They tease Geoffrey about eating fast food.
   ....
3. People judge him because of his strong Liverpool accent.
   ....
4. Family background, education and accent define social status.
   ....
5. Some chavs parked an old banger in my mother's front garden.
   ....
6. A business tycoon is buying the palace and its land.
   ....

4 British society. Ergänzen Sie den Text mit den fehlenden Wörtern!

chavs aristocrats stereotype toffs celebrities class system snob

You can still find examples of the traditional 1. .... in Britain. There is a monarchy and a long list of 2. ...., including dukes, earls and barons. However, many of these people have a lot less money than the richest 3. ...., who often like to buy old country palaces and live like royalty. The lower upper class and the upper middle class are sometimes called 4. .... The stereotypical upper class person is posh, known as a 5. .... These people speak what is called "Queen's" or "Oxford" English, use outdated words like "ghastly" or "jolly" and tend to have old-fashioned manners. At the opposite end of the spectrum, 6. .... are part of today's underclass, and there are just as many jokes about them as there are about the upper classes. The common 7. .... about these people is that they have strong regional accents and always wear tracksuits, trainers and a lot of cheap jewellery.

British manners

In general, most Brits are rather **private** people who like **to keep themselves to themselves** – unless they have had a bit too much to drink, perhaps! Much better examples of typical manners are shown by the polite and reserved character played by Hugh Grant in many romantic comedies and the famous **stiff upper lip** of the Queen, who would never express her emotions openly in a crisis.

Politeness and respect for **privacy** are both very important in Britain. The Brits do not like to "make a scene" and will **avoid** confrontation unless absolutely necessary. For example, nobody likes to hear long phone conversations on the train, but the Brits are unlikely to say anything. They will just shake their heads and **tut disapprovingly**. One thing that does drive them mad is **queue jumping**; this is **unforgivable**!

Brits say "sorry" a lot, even when someone else does something wrong. For example, if you walk into someone by accident, they will probably say, "Sorry!" And if you don't understand what someone says, just ask: "Sorry?"

A stiff upper lip?

The original poster

Compared to Southern Europeans and Americans, the British might seem unemotional and cold with their reserved and **resilient** nature and dry humour. However, be careful with **stereotypes**! Hippy culture also made it to the UK, and a more open, emotional culture has developed ever since.

One slogan has become an icon for the very British attitude of the stiff upper lip: "Keep calm and **carry on**!" This poster was created to motivate the nation during World War Two, but it was never used at the time. Some 70 years later, it shows that British reserve and understatement still live on – and are more fashionable than ever!

Laughter is the best medicine

British humour is famous all over the world, and in many ways it is quite special. You probably know several British shows like *Mr Bean*, *Little Britain* or *Monty Python*. This kind of comedy shows how the British love the absurd as well as general **silliness** and sarcasm. Sometimes the way they laugh at themselves and at each other can even be quite cruel. On the other hand, you could say that silliness and **self-deprecation** are important **antidotes** to the stereotypical British reserve. Both are easy to find in the stand-up comedy of Billy Connolly and Michael McIntyre, two of Britain's most successful entertainers. Irony also goes hand in hand with British understatement: Brits often say the opposite to what they mean, and they do so without laughing. Such dry humour can make it difficult to know whether they are being serious or not.

The English language is very flexible, so **native speakers** love to play with words in everyday conversation and **banter**. In particular, there are many words that sound the same but are spelled differently. You will find lots of **puns** in newspapers and magazines. This can be a fun way to learn English! Here is a classic pun – can you work out the joke?

Time flies like an arrow. Fruit flies like a banana.

private	*hier*: zurückhaltend, reserviert
to keep oneself to oneself	für sich bleiben
stiff upper lip	unerschütterliche Haltung, *wörtl.:* steife Oberlippe
privacy	Privatsphäre
to avoid	vermeiden
to tut disapprovingly	missbilligend schnalzen
queue jumping	Vordrängeln
unforgivable	unverzeihlich
resilient	zäh, unverwüstlich
stereotype	Kilschee, Vorurteil
to carry on	weitermachen
silliness	Albernheit
self-deprecation	Selbstironie
antidote	*hier:* Gegenmittel
native speaker	Muttersprachler(in)
banter	Wortgeplänkel
pun	Wortspiel

1 Jokes. Wie lautet die zweite Hälfte des Witzes? Ordnen Sie zu!

1. ☐ I've decided to sell my vacuum cleaner.
2. ☐ What is black and white, and red all over?
3. ☐ I'm on a whisky diet.
4. ☐ What do you get if you cross a kangaroo with a sheep?
5. ☐ Two fish are in a tank.
6. ☐ I slept like a log last night.

a) A newspaper.
b) I've already lost three days.
c) I woke up in the fireplace.
d) A woolly jumper.
e) It was only collecting dust.
f) One says, "How do you drive this thing?"

2 Puns in the press. Vervollständigen Sie die Schlagzeilen mit den fehlenden Wörtern und schreiben Sie unten die Wörter auf, die im Wortspiel ersetzt wurden!

wurst chew rain sand shelf toupee nappy busyness

1. Drip, drip, hooray! Queen celebrates .... lasting 60 years.
2. .... and glorious! Kate Middleton expecting baby.
3. Germans .... at penalties. England better from the spot.
4. It had to be ....! Suarez bites ... again!
5. There will be hell ....: Donald Trump furious over wind farms.
6. Help is at ....: five people saved from a tiny tropical island.
7. I'm too busy! How can we get out of this .... trap?
8. .... respect. The world's most beautiful libraries.

1. ....
2. ....
3. ....
4. ....
5. ....
6. ....
7. ....
8. ....

3 Everyday English. Was sagt man am besten in den folgenden Situationen?

1. ☐ A small child walks in front of you.
2. ☐ You didn't hear what someone said.
3. ☐ You hit someone with your umbrella.
4. ☐ You don't understand someone.
5. ☐ You want to get someone's attention.

a) "Excuse me!"
b) "Oh, sorry!"
c) "Watch out!"
d) "Pardon?"
e) "Sorry?"

CAPITAL PUNISHMENT!

A classic pun

4 Quotes about the British. Ergänzen Sie die Sätze mit den fehlenden Wörtern und entdecken Sie ein paar witzige Zitate über die Briten!

trust embarrassment America language language right bad cuisine only breakfast class happy

1. The land of .... and .... (Julian Barnes)
2 They are the .... people who like to be told how .... things are. (Winston Churchill)
3. You cannot .... people who have such bad .... (Jacques Chirac)
4. England and .... are two countries separated by the same .... (George Bernard Shaw)
5. .... is the British .... (William Golding)
6. They do not want to be ....; they want to be .... (Quentin Crisp)

Tastier than you think

The United Kingdom is not well known for good food. In fact, it is famous for bad food! However, the country that gave the world star chefs like Jamie Oliver and Heston Blumenthal actually has an enormous selection of regional specialities that are definitely worth trying.

Fish and chips

The best-known British dish is probably fish and chips. While seafood and potatoes have certainly been popular for a long time, the first fish and chip shop (or "chippy") did not open until 1860. Today, more than 10,000 chippies serve the nation with **battered** fish and portions of thick chips, traditionally covered in salt and vinegar. You can also choose from a number of sauces, including tomato ketchup, mayonnaise, **tartare sauce** or even curry sauce. And how about a portion of **mushy peas** or **pickled** onions on the side?

Brits like to have their main meal in the evening when everyone is back home. Lunch is often just a sandwich or salad, and most people only eat cereal or toast in the morning. The famous cooked breakfast is limited to hotels or brunch, typically at the weekend. However, many cafés also sell an all-day breakfast for people on the move - sausage, bacon, eggs, beans and mushrooms!

Regional specialities

You can find many different delicious cakes in bakeries and tea shops all over Britain. Devon and Cornwall are famous for scones – small, plain cakes often baked with raisins or lavender. Scones served with thick cream and jam are the main component of the traditional "cream tea". Other counties have more **savoury** specialities, such as Yorkshire pudding (crispy baked batter – a must with roast beef), Lincolnshire and Cumberland sausage, Lancashire **hotpot** and Cornish **pasties**. And you will find **superb** cheeses all over Britain, including Cheddar, Wensleydale and Stilton. However, some of the best food in the UK came with its international community. You can enjoy fantastic Asian dishes almost anywhere, and one of the nation's favourite meals is chicken tikka masala – a fusion of spicy meat and a creamy sauce that was invented in Glasgow!

Pubs

Britain has thousands of pubs ("public houses"). Ask the locals about the best place to drink or just choose a pub with a name that makes you smile. And for traditional British food, why not try some **pub grub** like **bangers and mash** or steak and kidney pie? All pubs sell a large selection of beer and cider, and some also serve local or even **home-brewed** varieties. And if you like to mix lemonade with your beer, just ask for a "shandy".

Whisky or tea?

Scottish whisky ("Scotch") is perhaps the most famous alcoholic drink from Britain. Scotland has five distinct whisky regions and hundreds of distilleries that each produce "the water of life" with a special flavour.

The Brits love their tea and will have a "cuppa" to wake up in the morning or relax. In fact, the British enjoy about 165 million cups of tea every day! So if someone offers to put the kettle on, say yes – it's an important part of being **sociable**. In the past, afternoon tea was served between 4 and 5 p.m. with cake and biscuits, but nowadays there is no set time for a relaxing **brew**!

battered	im Rührteig frittiert
tartare sauce	Remouladensoße
mushy peas *pl*	Erbsenpüree
pickled	eingelegt
savoury	herzhaft, salzig
hotpot	Eintopf
pasty	Pastete, Teigtasche
superb	hervorragend
pub grub	Kneipenessen
bangers and mash	Bratwürste mit Kartoffelbrei
home-brewed	hausgebraut
sociable	gesellig, freundlich
brew	eine Tasse Tee (Gebräu)

1 In the pub. Ergänzen Sie den Text mit den fehlenden Wörtern!

waitress round order served bar tip barmaid

When you go to the pub in Britain, you have to 1. .... your drinks from the bar and carry them to your table. There are no reserved seats for regular guests, but you will often see the same people sitting or standing in their favourite place. Regulars might also sit at the 2. ...., where they can talk to the barman or 3. .... all night long. Groups of friends take it in turns to buy a 4. ...., and it is usually bad manners to leave the pub before you have had your turn to buy everyone else a drink. If the person behind the bar is very friendly, you can 5. .... him or her by inviting him to "have one for yourself". The rules are a little different if you decide to eat at a pub: you will often be seated in a different area, and you will be 6. .... by a waiter or 7. .... You do not have to tip waiters in very informal restaurants and cafés, but otherwise you should give about 10% for good service.

2 Slang. Wie heißen folgende Lebensmittel in der Umgangssprache? Ordnen Sie zu!

1. ☐ sausage	a) banger
2. ☐ sandwich	b) grub
3. ☐ toasted sandwich	c) plonk
4. ☐ salad	d) sarnie
5. ☐ beer	e) spud
6. ☐ wine	f) liquid bread
7. ☐ food (in general)	g) rabbit food
8. ☐ potato	h) toastie

Fancy something different? Scan the QR code to download some British recipes!

3 Regional food. Welche Spezialitäten aus dem Text werden beschrieben?

1. A meat and vegetable stew that will keep you warm. ....
2. A pie filled with meat and vegetables. ....
3. A spiral of meat seasoned with fragrant herbs. ....
4. A round baked treat served with sweet cream and jam. ....
5. A savoury side dish made from milk, flour and eggs. ....
6. A creamy and spicy British-Asian dish. ....

4 Fun food facts. Welche Antwort ist richtig? Kreuzen Sie an!

1. The Earl of Sandwich asked for meat to be put between two slices of bread so that he could keep his hands clean when playing what game?
   a) ❑ croquet b) ❑ snooker c) ❑ cards

2. Which of these towns did not give its name to a type of British cheese?
   a) ❑ Wensleydale b) ❑ Bournemouth c) ❑ Leicester

3. Queen Elizabeth I made a law that led to this classic combination with roast lamb.
   a) ❑ mint sauce b) ❑ tomato sauce c) ❑ tartare sauce

4. What can you buy for dessert in some Scottish chippies, deep fried in batter?
   a) ❑ a chocolate bar b) ❑ a banana c) ❑ ice cream

5. Each year at Wimbledon, around 28 tonnes of these are eaten with cream.
   a) ❑ blueberries b) ❑ strawberries c) ❑ blackberries

6. One reason why the Romans wanted to invade Britain is because they had heard the sea was full of these delicious animals.
   a) ❑ oysters b) ❑ tuna c) ❑ octopus

7. What percentage of British people put milk in their tea?
   a) ❑ 70% b) ❑ 90% c) ❑ 98%

British sports and the beautiful game

Did you know that many popular team sports like football, rugby, cricket and hockey were born in the United Kingdom? Other examples of traditional British sports include golf, boxing, lawn tennis, table tennis, badminton and snooker – quite a long list!

Football is the nation's favourite sport. One in two people in Britain **regularly** watch matches on television and all sorts of people love to have a friendly **kickabout**. Although clubs such as Arsenal, Chelsea, Manchester United and Manchester City are very **successful**, England has only one international title: it won the World Cup back in 1966. Scotland, Wales and Northern Ireland usually do not qualify for important **tournaments**, but it's the taking part that counts!

Do the Brits really love sport? They actually are one of the fattest nations in Europe, and a typical person spends only 50 minutes a week doing sport. But perhaps that makes sense after all: the traditional places to watch a football match are in the pub with friends or at home on the sofa with a beer and an Indian takeaway!

Rugby – "a real man's game"

People say that rugby was born almost 200 years ago when a student at Rugby School decided to pick up the ball and run with it during a game of football. It is a much more aggressive game than football, and players are often **injured**. The sport is more popular in Scotland, Northern Ireland and Wales, where it is also the national sport, but there are teams all over the UK. Rugby fans love the Six Nations Championship early each year, when Northern Ireland joins up with the Republic of Ireland to play its three neighbours as well as France and Italy. There is some **rivalry** between the British teams, but everyone is on the same side when it comes to beating the French!

Seasonal sports

Wimbledon, the world's oldest tennis tournament, is a highlight of the summer for many Brits, and in 2013 they finally found a champion in the Scotsman Andy Murray. Another important event in the sporting calendar is the Ashes – a series of cricket matches between England and Australia. Professional cricket is only played in the Commonwealth countries. For something faster, horse racing and motor racing are very popular on television and at the **track**. If you visit Britain, why not try to win some money at the **greyhound** races? You could be a little richer after "a day at the dogs" if you are lucky when **placing bets**!

Unusual sports

The British can be eccentric, and this is especially true when it comes to some of their local sporting traditions. From rolling cheese down a dangerous hill to playing football in the river, **mud** wrestling, **shin-kicking** and even **gurning**, they seem to make anything a sport. But there are more serious traditions, too. Scotland's Highland games have a long history, for example. The most famous event here is **tossing the caber** – but there are many athletic sports as well. Ireland has four Gaelic games. The most popular are Gaelic football and **hurling**, which go back to Celtic times.

regularly	regelmäßig	**greyhound**	Windhund
kickabout	Kicken	**to place a bet**	eine Wette abgeben
successful	erfolgreich	**mud**	Schlamm
tournament	Turnier	**shin-kicking**	Schienbeintreten
injured	verletzt	**gurning**	Grimassenschneiden
rivalry	Rivalität	**tossing the caber**	Baumstammwerfen
track	*hier:* Rennbahn	**hurling**	irisches Hockey

1 The rules of the game. Welche Sportart wird beschrieben?

1. Two teams of 15 play for 80 minutes. They have to put the ball on the ground behind the other team's line, which is called scoring a try. They can also kick the ball over the bar. ....
2. Two players hit balls of seven colours on a table with a white ball. If a ball goes into one of the six pockets, they can have another go. ....
3. This sport is for two or four players and has a shuttlecock instead of a ball. The winner is usually the first to score 15. ....
4. Two teams of 11 try to score goals by kicking the ball into the other team's net. A match usually lasts for 90 minutes, but sometimes there is extra time and a penalty shoot-out. ....

2 Modern sporting heroes and heroines. Wissen Sie, wofür diese britischen Sportstars berühmt sind? Ordnen Sie zu!

1. ☐ Ryan Giggs
2. ☐ Sir Bradley Wiggins
3. ☐ Sir Steve Redgrave
4. ☐ Lewis Hamilton
5. ☐ David Beckham
6. ☐ Ellie Simmonds
7. ☐ Jessica Ennis

a) This swimmer has over 30 gold medals and first took part in the Paralympic Games at the age of 13.
b) Britain's greatest Olympian – this rower won five gold medals in five Olympic Games between 1984 and 2000.
c) This racing driver won the Formula One championship in 2008 and 2014.
d) This athlete won the Olympic heptathlon *(Siebenkampf)* in 2012.
e) This Olympic cyclist was the first British person to win the Tour de France.
f) This Welsh footballer played for Manchester United more than 950 times.
g) This footballer was captain of the English team 59 times and scored goals in three World Cups.

Culture and the arts

Die Kulturlandschaft im Land von Shakespeare, den Beatles oder Alfred Hitchcock ist so bunt und vielfältig, dass es hier unmöglich ist, alle Klassiker und Weltstars zu würdigen. Zum enormen Einfluss britischer Kultur trägt nicht zuletzt auch die Weltsprache Englisch bei, die es britischen Künstlern erlaubt, rund um den Erdball ein großes Publikum anzusprechen.

Sicher kennen Sie einige britische Künstler, Romane oder Bands. Und wer ist kein Fan von modernen Klassikern wie *James Bond* oder *Harry Potter*? Aber wussten Sie, dass die Briten pro Kopf mehr Musik kaufen als jede andere Nation? Oder dass das Theaterstück *The Mousetrap* in London seit 1952 jeden Tag auf dem Spielplan steht? Und es gibt noch viel mehr zu entdecken und zu erleben!

Literature – a world of words

There is a good chance that you have already read a crime story by Agatha Christie, the world's best-selling **novelist**. Or maybe a play by William Shakespeare, who many believe to be the world's greatest **playwright**? Or how about *The Lord of the Rings*?

Early writers

The Medieval **epic poem** *Beowulf* is celebrated as one of the first great works of literature in Britain, but the father of English literature was Geoffrey Chaucer, who lived in the second half of the 14th century. He is best known for *The Canterbury Tales*, a collection of **saucy** stories that have inspired other writers ever since.

William Shakespeare, otherwise known simply as "the Bard", is Britain's national poet. We know surprisingly little about his life, but people believe he was born in Stratford-upon-Avon in 1564. He wrote 154 sonnets and 37 plays, some of the most popular being *Hamlet*, *Romeo and Juliet* and *A Midsummer Night's Dream*. Shakespeare used to act in his own productions at the Globe Theatre in London. Nowadays, unlike in Shakespeare's days, the female characters are actually played by women!

Classic novels

One of the first British novels, Daniel Defoe's *Robinson Crusoe*, was published in 1719. Sir Walter Scott (1771–1832) is another famous early novelist. He is best known for *Ivanhoe*, which brought folk hero Robin Hood face to face with evil Norman invaders. Even more popular is Jane Austen (1775–1817), whose **witty** and entertaining romantic novels are still fresh today – for example *Pride and Prejudice* and *Sense and Sensibility*.

Charles Dickens (1812–70), a master of drama and dialogue, was enormously successful during the Victorian period. His unforgettable characters are still known and loved by millions. If you have never read any Dickens, an excellent place to start is *A Christmas Carol*. Other **outstanding** Victorian authors were the three Brontë sisters, George Eliot and Thomas Hardy.

There are so many great authors and prominent poets from the United Kingdom that it is impossible to focus on just a few. Recipients of the Nobel Prize in Literature include Rudyard Kipling (1907), T. S. Eliot (1948), Winston Churchill (1953), Harold Pinter (2005) and Doris Lessing (2007).

Popular genres

Murder mysteries are one of the most popular types of **fiction** in the UK. Scotsman Sir Arthur Conan Doyle (1859–1930) created the iconic detective *Sherlock Holmes* in 1886, but the character became so successful that the author had to kill him off in order to focus on other work. Later crime writers include Agatha Christie, Colin Dexter and Ruth Rendell, to name but a few.
Fantasy and science fiction were also born in the 1800s with Mary Shelley's *Frankenstein* (1818). H. G. Wells's *The War of the Worlds* (1898) is a science fiction classic, and who hasn't seen the films based on J. R. R. Tolkien's epic *The Lord of the Rings* (1937) – the ultimate in fantasy fiction? Not to forget Orwell's **disturbing** *Nineteen Eighty-Four* (1949) – "Big Brother is watching you!" – or Huxley's *A Brave New World* (1932). More recent fantasy writers include Terry Pratchett and Philip Pullman.

British children's fiction is a treat for the imagination, from *Alice's Adventures in Wonderland* (1865) by Lewis Carroll to *The Chronicles of Narnia* by C. S. Lewis and the magical stories of Roald Dahl and Dick King-Smith. And let's not forget J. K. Rowling's *Harry Potter* – a series so successful that the author became the first person ever to earn a billion from writing books!

novelist	Romanautor(in)	**outstanding**	hervorragend
playwright	Dramatiker(in)	**recipient**	Empfänger(in)
epic poem	Heldengedicht	**murder mystery**	Krimi
saucy	keck	**fiction**	Belletristik
witty	geistreich, witzig	**disturbing**	verstörend

1 Famous Shakespeare quotations. Welche Figur hat das gesagt? Ordnen Sie die Zitate zu!

Juliet Hamlet Lady Macbeth Mark Anthony Richard III Shylock

1. To be, or not to be: that is the question. ....
2. A horse, a horse, my kingdom for a horse! ....
3. My only love sprung from my only hate. ....
4. Friends, Romans, countrymen, lend me your ears. ....
5. The pound of flesh which I demand. ....
6. What's done cannot be undone. ....

2 Translation. Übersetzen Sie folgende Sätze ins Englische!

1. Viele Meisterwerke der Literatur sind für Kino und Fernsehen adaptiert worden.

   ....

2. Miss Marple ist eine beliebte Figur von Agatha Christie, die der Polizei gern hilft.

   ....

3. Wir wissen überraschend wenig über Shakespeare und sein Privatleben.

   ....

4. Dickens war unglaublich erfolgreich in der viktorianischen Zeit.

   ....

5. Doyle hat insgesamt 56 Geschichten und vier Romane über Holmes geschrieben.

   ....

3 Crime authors. Welcher Autor hat welche Krimifigur erschaffen? Ordnen Sie zu!

1. ☐ Hercule Poirot	a) Sir Arthur Conan Doyle
2. ☐ Inspector Wexford	b) P. D. James
3. ☐ Inspector Morse	c) Colin Dexter
4. ☐ Sherlock Holmes	d) Ian Rankin
5. ☐ Inspector Rebus	e) Agatha Christie
6. ☐ Inspector Dalgliesh	f) Ruth Rendell

4 Prepositions. Vervollständigen Sie den Text mit den fehlenden Präpositionen!

Have you read anything 1. .... the best-selling modern writers 2. .... Britain? 3. .... Shakespeare and Agatha Christie, Barbara Cartland has sold the most books. She published over 700 romantic novels 4. .... the twentieth century. Or perhaps as a child you used to read *The Famous Five* or *The Secret Seven* by the ever-popular Enid Blyton? Going back 5. .... adult fiction, all 29 of the romantic novels by Jackie Collins, the sister 6. .... Joan, have been bestsellers. Popular authors of thrillers include Ken Follett, John Le Carré and Frederick Forsyth, while several novels 7. .... both Nick Hornby and Ian McEwan have been turned 8. .... films.

5 Famous novels. Welches Buch wird beschrieben? Ordnen Sie zu!

1. ☐ *Lord of the Flies* William Golding
2. ☐ *A Christmas Carol* Charles Dickens
3. ☐ *Animal Farm* George Orwell
4. ☐ *Pride and Prejudice* Jane Austen
5. ☐ *Robinson Crusoe* Daniel Defoe
6. ☐ *The Time Machine* H. G. Wells
7. ☐ *Gulliver's Travels* Jonathan Swift

a) The Bennet sisters meet Mr Bingley and Mr Darcy, two wealthy gentlemen who are searching for a wife.
b) A satire about an English traveller who visits strange lands.
c) As the year comes to an end, a mean old man is visited by ghosts who teach him what it really means to be human.
d) An inventor builds a device that allows him to visit the very distant future.
e) A group of boys arrive on an uninhabited island after a plane crash and attempt to live by their own rules.
f) All are equal, but some are more equal than others in this parable of communism.
g) A young man tries to make money by adventuring at sea but ends up stranded on a remote island.

The sound of music

You probably have a lot of English songs on your favourite playlist because some of the world's most famous singers and bands over the last 50 years have come from Britain. Music is a big part of life everywhere, but it is especially important in the UK. Here people buy more singles and albums per person than in any other country. And on karaoke nights all over the country, you'll hear people singing much-loved British **anthems** such as *Angels* by Robbie Williams, *Bohemian Rhapsody* by Queen, *Don't Go Breaking My Heart* by Elton John, *Karma Chameleon* by Culture Club and *Chasing Cars* by Snow Patrol – **the** more **eclectic**, **the** better!

The Beatles

The Beatles began a new **chapter** in pop music history and became one of the greatest groups of all time. The band started playing in clubs in Liverpool and Hamburg in 1960. Just a few years later, John Lennon, Paul McCartney, George Harrison and Ringo Starr were stars on both sides of the Atlantic and the most important band of the **decade**. You could even call the Fab Four the first boy band – groups of screaming fans followed them everywhere. The Beatles sold more albums than any other British band, and they also made five films before their **break-up** in 1970.

Britpop

About twenty years after the Fab Four, a new style of music **appeared** in Britain in reaction to dance music and American grunge bands like Nirvana. Britpop dominated the charts in the 1990s with innovative groups like Suede and Pulp, who wrote songs about British life and sang in regional accents. The two main bands were Blur from the South and Oasis from the North. Britpop had a strong **influence** on later groups like Coldplay and also **set the stage** for a new **wave** of British pop music – from the Spice Girls to Adele and James Blunt.

Live music is big business and there is a growing number of festivals each year. The biggest festivals in Britain are in Glastonbury, Reading and Leeds, but there are hundreds of others and some of them are even free!

Musicals

In the late nineteenth century, Gilbert and Sullivan wrote 14 comic operas, including *The Pirates of Penzance* and *The Mikado*, which are still popular today. Their modern **equivalent** is Sir Andrew Lloyd Webber, who has written 13 musicals. Some of these have been playing in the West End – London's theatre district – and around the world for many years. Almost everyone will know a song or two from *Jesus Christ Superstar*, *Evita*, *Cats* or *The Phantom of the Opera*.

Classical music

Great British **composers** include Henry Purcell, Georg Friedrich Handel (a German who became British), Edward Elgar and Benjamin Britten. Karl Jenkins, a Welsh musician, is one of the most popular composers alive. **Conductor** Sir Simon Rattle and violinist Nigel Kennedy are famous worldwilde for making classical music more **accessible**. The BBC Proms concerts in summer are also very popular. Most concerts take place at the Royal Albert Hall in London and **are broadcast** on television and radio. This is the world's biggest music festival, and it is now more than 120 years old!

anthem	*hier:* Kracher, Hymne	**to set the stage**	die Voraussetzungen schaffen
the..., the...	je ..., desto ...	**wave**	Welle
eclectic	bunt gemischt	**equivalent**	Entsprechung
chapter	Kapitel	**composer**	Komponist(in)
decade	Jahrzehnt	**conductor**	Dirigent(in)
break-up	Trennung, Auflösung	**accessible**	zugänglich
to appear	erscheinen	**to be broadcast**	gesendet werden
influence	Einfluss		

1 Rolling Stones or Beatles? Unterstreichen Sie die richtige Variante!

1. In the 1960s, music lovers on **both** / **each** sides of the Atlantic defined themselves by whether they were fans of the Beatles or the Rolling Stones.
2. The two bands **use to** / **used to** say that there was no rivalry between them.
3. Although the two groups got **over** / **along**, they also tried to outperform *(übertreffen)* each other.
4. The Stones had a wilder image, with long hair and unusual **outfits** / **dressing**.
5. Fans of the Beatles were even louder and **exciteder** / **more excited** than fans of the Rolling Stones.
6. The Beatles **broke up** / **have broken up** in 1970, but the Rolling Stones are still going strong.

2 Match up. Zu welchem Genre gehören die Stücke und von wem stammen sie?

classical **pop** **soul** **heavy metal** **punk rock** **Britpop** **ska** **rock**

1. ☐ Enigma Variations	....	a) Pet Shop Boys
2. ☐ The Number of the Beast	....	b) Madness
3. ☐ Anarchy in the UK	....	c) Edward Elgar
4. ☐ Country House	....	d) Iron Maiden
5. ☐ It's a Sin	....	e) Blur
6. ☐ Rehab	....	f) Pink Floyd
7. ☐ House of Fun	....	g) Sex Pistols
8. ☐ We Don't Need No Education	....	h) Amy Winehouse

3 Spot the mistakes. Unterstreichen Sie die sechs Fehler im Text und verbessern Sie sie!

The Beatles begun a new chapter in pop music history and became one of the most great groups of all time. The band started playing in clubs in Liverpool and Hamburg in 1960. Just a few years later, they were stars on both sides of the Atlantic. You could even call the Fab Four the first boy band – groups of screaming fans followed them every where. The Beatles selled more albums then any other British band, and they also made five films. All four group members had a sucessful solo career after the break-up in 1970.

1. .... 2. ....

3. .... 4. ....

5. .... 6. ....

4 Music crossword. Welche Begriffe zum Thema Musik werden gesucht?

1. The person who directs an orchestra, e.g. Simon Rattle and Herbert von Karajan.
2. A musical event that lasts for several days, often taking place outdoors.
3. Famous hits to which many people know the words. Each country also has a national one.
4. Someone who writes music, especially classical works or film scores.
5. A series of summer concerts organized by the BBC.
6. The list of the most popular and most successful songs or albums, updated each week.
7. Singing the words to recorded pop music or music videos, often in a bar or pub.

Stage and screen

British cinema has a long tradition, from Charlie Chaplin to Guy Ritchie, and it is big business. Many television dramas from the UK are also well known in other countries. For example, did you know that the crime series *Midsomer Murders* with Inspector Barnaby is one of Angela Merkel's favourite shows?

British cinema

The golden age of British cinema was in the mid-twentieth century, and classics like *Brief Encounter* (1945), *Lawrence of Arabia* (1962) or *The Life of Brian* (1979) are still enjoyed today. Modern films are often about very British topics: Scottish subculture in *Trainspotting*, for example, or the 1984 **miners' strike** in *Billy Elliot*. British comedies are loved around the world, especially romantic comedies ("romcoms") like *Bridget Jones's Diary* or *Shakespeare in Love*, horror **spoofs** like *Shaun of the Dead* and animated films like *Chicken Run* and the *Wallace & Gromit* series. The world's longest film series is also a British comedy: 31 *Carry On* films – *Ist ja irre* in German – appeared between 1958 and 1992.

James Bond

Author Ian Fleming created Britain's most famous **spy** back in 1952. Since then, six actors have played the cult role in some of the world's best-loved action films. In 2012 *Skyfall*, the twenty-third **instalment** of the series, broke a record by making more money in British cinemas than any other film in history. The first Bond was Sean Connery, the charming Scotsman with style and good looks. Roger Moore was also a popular 007 – a lovable **rogue** – even though the actor is actually afraid of guns! Daniel Craig took up the role of Bond in 2006, when the films also became much darker in tone. In total, Her Majesty's secret agent has killed more than 350 people and slept with more than 50 women – quite an exciting life!

Television

Filming Sherlock *in London*

The British Broadcasting Corporation is the world's oldest and largest national **broadcasting company**. Many people believe that the BBC produces the world's best news programmes, documentaries and dramas. Some of its latest hit shows are *Sherlock* and *Doctor Who*. However, other British broadcasting companies also make series that have won top awards, such as *Downton Abbey* and *Prime Suspect*.

Soaps always have the largest **audiences**. These programmes can show you a **slice** of British culture today, but it goes without saying that they are not very realistic! The most popular soap on British television is *Coronation Street*. It celebrated its 50th anniversary in 2010 and is now the world's longest-running soap. It is set near Manchester with many likeable characters, whereas London-based *EastEnders* is famous for its **doom and gloom**.

Dressing up for a pantomime

Theatre

Around half of all theatre ticket sales in Britain are for productions in London. Since 1952, there have been more than 25,000 **performances** of Agatha Christie's play *The Mousetrap* in the capital – another world record! But **murder mysteries** are not the only popular genre. From Shakespearean tragedies to lively musicals, there is something for everyone. If you are in Britain over Christmas, why not try a pantomime? These are adaptations of well-known stories for all the family, with famous celebrities playing Cinderella or Aladdin, lots of singing, cross-dressing and general **silliness** – all part of the tradition!

miners' strike	Bergarbeiterstreik	**audience**	Publikum, Zuschauer
spoof	Parodie	**slice**	*hier:* Ausschnitt
spy	Spion(in)	**doom and gloom**	Pessimismus, Untergangsstimmung
instalment	*hier*: Fortsetzung	**performance**	Aufführung
rogue	Schlingel	**murder mystery**	Krimi
broadcasting company	Rundfunkgesellschaft	**silliness**	Albernheit

1 Translation quiz. Übersetzen Sie die Wörter ins Englische und enträtseln Sie das Lösungswort!

1. Publikum _ _ _ _ _ _ □ _
2. Bergarbeiter (pl.) _ □ _ _ _ _
3. Fortsetzung _ □ _ _ _ _ _ □ _ _
4. Sendung _ _ _ _ _ _ □ _ _
5. Seifenoper _ _ □ _

Hidden word: _ _ _ _ _ _

2 Present Perfect or Simple Past? Ergänzen Sie die richtige Verbform!

be play watch see produce pay

1. The Chancellor .... her favourite British murder mystery last night.
2. Britain .... a lot of popular comedy films over the years.
3. Millions of people .... *Coronation Street* over the years.
4. British actors .... most of the characters in the *Harry Potter* films.
5. Every household .... the television licence fee in 2014.
6. Did you realize that the ugly sister in the pantomime .... actually a man?

3 True or false? Welche Aussagen sind korrekt? Kreuzen Sie an!

1. In Shakespeare's times, men played female roles on the stage. ❑
2. Male celebrities often play women in pantomimes. ❑
3. There are more James Bond films than any other series. ❑
4. Roger Moore was the first actor to play James Bond. ❑
5. *EastEnders* is one of the most popular television shows in Britain. ❑
6. Most theatre productions are in London. ❑
7. The typical British person watches four hours of television a day. ❑
8. It is traditional for a character to die in a soap on Christmas Day. ❑

4 British sitcoms. Welche Fernsehsendungen werden beschrieben? Ordnen Sie zu!

1. ☐ *The Office*
2. ☐ *The Vicar of Dibley*
3. ☐ *Only Fools and Horses*
4. ☐ *Outnumbered*
5. ☐ *Fawlty Towers*
6. ☐ *Keeping Up Appearances*

a) Two brothers in Peckham, London, try to find clever ways to make money.
b) Two parents have a hard time looking after three children with very strong personalities.
c) A chaotic hotel manager and his posh wife look after difficult guests.
d) Hyacinth Bucket tries to hide her working-class family from her middle-class neighbours.
e) A member of the church with some bad habits finds her place in an unusual village community.
f) A terrible manager tells the camera how wonderful he and his company are.

> J. K. Rowling asked for British actors when her *Harry Potter* books were made into films. The credits therefore read like a "who's who" of stage and screen in the United Kingdom.

5 Film and theatre quiz. Kreuzen Sie die richtige Antwort an!

1. Which British film won the most Oscars?
   a) ❑ Slumdog Millionaire
   b) ❑ The English Patient
   c) ❑ Gandhi

2. Which actor and director is famous for his Shakespeare films?
   a) ❑ Kenneth Branagh
   b) ❑ Richard Attenborough
   c) ❑ John Schlesinger

3. Which play by Shakespeare is the most produced theatre play ever?
   a) ❑ Romeo and Juliet
   b) ❑ Macbeth
   c) ❑ Hamlet

4. How many theatre productions are there in London each year?
   a) ❑ around 10,000
   b) ❑ around 12,000
   c) ❑ around 18,000

Art and design

Historic castles, palaces and a variety of museums across Britain allow visitors to admire large collections of fine paintings and sculptures from around the world as well as the buildings themselves. There are also wonderful **landscaped gardens** such as those at Hampton Court and Blenheim Palace – the birthplace of Winston Churchill. Modern design is just as diverse, from the lively **contemporary** art scene in Glasgow to the exclusive fashion labels on Savile Row in London's Mayfair.

Fine art

The biggest names in British art history are from the Romantic period and later. Two of the greatest are John Constable and William Turner, both of whom painted landscapes in the early 1800s. The former focused on detail and precise composition whereas the latter preferred the **bold** use of colour and a more innovative technique. Like many great artists, Turner had an eccentric personality and refused to follow conventions. His obsession with light and colour led to paintings that were almost impressionist in style and even influenced his last words: "The sun is god." When he died, Turner left his oil paintings to the nation, and one of the biggest prizes in the art world carries his name **to this day**. The Romantic poet William Blake was also an important artist. His drawing of Sir Isaac Newton inspired an enormous statue of the scientist outside the British Library, which was created by Scottish sculptor Sir Eduardo Paolozzi in 1995.

In the early twentieth century, **art nouveau** and later art deco became fashionable with prominent designers such as Charles Rennie Mackintosh and Clarice Cliff. Popular painters from the twentieth century include Anglo-Irish Francis Bacon, L. S. Lowry and Lucian Freud, the German-born grandson of Sigmund Freud.

Newton statue by Paolozzi

Modern art

Sharks, cows and **doves** in tanks of formaldehyde, an unmade bed surrounded by rubbish and a **skull** covered in diamonds worth £50 million – is it art? It is if you ask Damien Hirst and Tracey Emin, two of the most successful members of the Young British Artists, a movement that began in the 1980s. They aim to **push the boundaries** of modern art, and their work remains highly controversial. You can see examples at the Tate Modern, a **converted** power station and the most visited contemporary art museum in the world. A cult figure among the British public is Banksy, the most famous graffiti artist there is, who originally comes from Bristol. His real identity remains a mystery. Another favourite is the playful Grayson Perry, whose colourful creations include ceramic vases and urns. He is best known for dressing up as Clare, his alter ego, even when appearing on national television or collecting awards from Buckingham Palace!

Banksy graffiti mocking surveillance

Each corner of Trafalgar Square has a plinth, but there are only three statues – the fourth was never built. Since 1999, contemporary artists have been invited to display work on the fourth plinth with frequently amusing results. Members of the public have also appeared there: 2,400 people were given an hour each to do whatever they liked back in 2009.

landscaped garden	Landschaftsgarten
contemporary	zeitgenössisch
bold	gewagt
to this day	bis heute
art nouveau	Jugendstil
dove	weiße Taube
skull	Schädel
to push the boundaries	die Grenzen ausloten
converted	umgebaut
plinth	Sockel
to display	zeigen, ausstellen

1 The British Museum. Übersetzen Sie die fehlenden Begriffe!

The British Museum is just a short 1. Spaziergang .... away from Oxford Street in central London. Dedicated to human history and culture, it is home to one of the greatest 2. Sammlungen .... in the world. There are over seven million items from six continents, covering all stages of 3. menschlich .... civilization. Some of the museum's most famous exhibits include the Rosetta Stone from Egypt and the Elgin Marbles from the Parthenon in Athens. The museum was 4. gegründet .... in 1753, and its growth in the following 5. Jahrhunderte .... reflects the expansion of the British Empire.

2 Word spiral. Lösen Sie das Rätsel!

1	2	3	4	5	6	7
22	23	24	25	26	27	8
21	36	37	38	39	28	9
20	35	42	41	40	29	10
19	34	33	32	31	30	11
18	17	16	15	14	13	12

1–12: Belonging to the same time.
12–16: The YBAs are the ... British Artists.
16–18: Turner's last words: "The sun is ...".
18–21: Banksy painted this animal, and Hirst put it in formaldehyde.
21–24: Tracey ... is often described as the enfant terrible of the British art scene.
24–30: Art ... was a popular style between 1880 and the First World War.
30–33: Grayson Perry is famous for his vases and ... .
33–37: The bone structure of the head.
37–42: ... Freud is a popular painter.

History and politics

Kommen Sie mit auf eine spannenden Reise durch die Geschichte! Wie wurde aus den einzelnen Völkern der britischen Inseln ein geeintes Land, das im neunzehnten Jahrhundert über das größte Weltreich herrschte, das jemals existierte? Bedeutende Monarchen wie Alfred der Große oder Elisabeth I. spielen dabei ebenso eine Rolle wie die britische Marine und verschiedenste Wellen von Einwanderern – von den Römern bis heute! Und die Kolonialgeschichte beeinflusst Großbritanniens Rolle in der Welt bis in die Gegenwart hinein – nicht nur durch die englische Sprache!

Rule, Britannia!

Early Britons

You can find **traces** of Late Stone Age life all over Britain and Ireland. The most famous example is Stonehenge, the mysterious circle of standing stones near Salisbury in South England, which is over 5,000 years old. But the ancient fishing village of Skara Brae in the Orkney Islands is just as unique. This is Europe's most complete **Neolithic** community, built when the sea around Scotland was a little warmer than it is today. The small stone houses here even had indoor toilets! When the climate cooled during the Iron Age, more people moved south. Hundreds of hill forts from this period can still be seen in England and Wales.

A Stone Age house in Skara Brae

The Romans

Boudicca's statue in London

Julius Caesar tried to invade Britain twice, but he was defeated by the bad weather! In 43 AD, however, the Romans finally crossed the sea from mainland Europe. A national heroine from this period is Boudicca, who led a successful **uprising** in 60 AD and burned down Colchester, the Roman capital of Britain. Struggles like this helped to give **tribes** of Britons a collective identity, but the Romans brought much more to the island. In addition to the name "Britannia", they established important cities such as Bath, Gloucester and Dover as well as today's capital, "Londinium".

The Anglo-Saxons

When the last Roman legions sailed away from Britain in 410 AD, the land was open to attack by tribes from the area north of Hadrian's Wall and from Ireland. At the same time, the Angles, Saxons and Jutes arrived from today's Germany and Denmark. It was the Anglo-Saxons that slowly became dominant, bringing a new language and culture to the British Isles. During the seventh century, they began

to convert to Christianity. Over time, the land of the Angles became known as "Eng-land", and today the English identify themselves as Anglo-Saxons as passionately as the Welsh, Scottish and Irish call themselves Celts.

The Vikings

Starting in 793 and for the next 250 years, Britain experienced countless **raids** from the Vikings. There were even Danish kings on the throne for three generations, but the Vikings are mainly remembered for their violence. In the late ninth century, the Anglo-Saxons all joined together under King Alfred the Great to fight the Nordic invaders.

A new English language, Middle English, was born after the Norman invasion as French words entered the vocabulary. Take food, for example: Saxon farmers raised cows, sheep and swine, but these animals were served to Norman rulers to eat as beef ("bœuf"), mutton ("mouton") and pork ("porc").

The Normans

Without doubt, the Norman **conquest** in 1066 was a turning point in British history. Harold II of England was the last ever Anglo-Saxon monarch, but the Duke of Normandy, William, believed the throne was his. William and his Norman armies de-feated Harold in the Battle of Hastings, described in detail on the famous Bayeux **Tapestry**. The Nor-mans **ruled** large parts of the British Isles with an iron fist, building impressive castles to control the lands violently taken from the Anglo-Saxons.

trace	Spur	**raid**	Angriff, Überfall
Neolithic	jungsteinzeitlich	**conquest**	Eroberung
uprising	Aufstand	**tapestry**	Wandteppich
tribe	Volksstamm	**to rule**	herrschen

1 Facts and figures. Unterstreichen Sie die richtige Variante!

1. Modern humans **inhabit** / **have inhabited** the British Isles for about 40,000 years.
2. Some cultures **were using** / **used** Stonehenge for rituals to remember the dead.
3. Emperor Claudius invaded Britain in 43 **BC** / **AD**.
4. Most Anglo-Saxon kingdoms gave their name to English **towns** / **counties**.
5. The Normans came from Normandy and were descendants of Viking **conquerors** / **neighbours**.
6. According to the Bayeux Tapestry, Harold was killed by an arrow in the **eye** / **heart**.
7. The Domesday Book of 1086 is a record of land and **property** / **people** in England.
8. The **Viking** / **Norman** invasion is one reason why English has so many words.
9. After the Norman conquest, **French** / **Norwegian** was spoken in England's courts for centuries.

2 Alfred the Great. Lesen Sie den Absatz über Alfred den Großen und übersetzen Sie die fehlenden Begriffe ins Englische!

King Alfred (849–99) is the only English 1. Herrscher .... known as "the Great". Anglo-Saxon England was divided into seven 2. Königreiche .... Alfred's family were the leaders of Wessex in the south. By 870, every other part of the country was controlled by 3. Wikinger .... from Denmark, who also wanted to take Wessex – the last independent kingdom. Alfred's family led a successful defence against the 4. Angreifer ....
After becoming king, Alfred negotiated an agreement with the Danes, and they shared the land. He then reorganized the army, established a navy and built many strong 5. Siedlungen .... in the south. He was also a wise king. He created a code of laws and understood the importance of education. In his late thirties, he learnt 6. Latein .... and translated books into the common language. Coins from the 890s 7. beschreiben .... him as "King of the English".

3 The Middle Ages. Welche Antwort ist richtig? Kreuzen Sie an!

1. In the legend of Robin Hood, Bad King John is the brother of Richard the Lionheart. He took the throne when Good King Richard went to fight ....
   a) ❑ Danish invaders b) ❑ Scottish rebels c) ❑ Muslims in Jerusalem

2. King John disagreed with the church and with the barons. He increased taxes and was cruel to the people of England. How did the barons stop him in 1215?
   a) ❑ They killed him. b) ❑ They led a revolution. c) ❑ They limited his power.

3. The Black Death killed millions of people in Europe in the 1300s – perhaps as much as half the population. What other name does it have in English?
   a) ❑ the pest b) ❑ the plague c) ❑ the infestation

4. Which was the most important destination for pilgrims in medieval England?
   a) ❑ Winchester Cathedral b) ❑ Canterbury Cathedral c) ❑ Gloucester Cathedral

5. After the Normans, the English throne went to the House of Plantagenet, which ruled from 1154 to 1485. What symbol was used by many of these rulers?
   a) ❑ castle b) ❑ unicorn c) ❑ three lions

6. Where in England can you find Sherwood Forest and a statue of Robin Hood?
   a) ❑ Nottinghamshire b) ❑ Northamptonshire c) ❑ Leicestershire

4 Translation quiz. Übersetzen Sie die Wörter ins Englische und enträtseln Sie das Lösungswort!

1. Volksstamm _ _ ☐ _ _
2. einzigartig _ ☐ _ _ _ _
3. Gewalt ☐ _ _ _ _ _ _ _
4. Überfall _ ☐ _ ☐
5. Wandteppich _ _ _ ☐ _ _ _ _

Hidden word: _ _ _ _ _ _

Henry VIII (1491-1547)

Britain's most notorious king is remembered for his six wives and his decision to turn his back on the Pope, creating the Church of England. Henry began to question the amount of money that was going to Rome – capital that he needed to finance his growing fleet of ships. He was also **determined** to have a male **heir** to protect the Tudor dynasty, but his first wife, Catherine of Aragon, gave him only one daughter. After breaking with the Vatican, Henry married his already pregnant **mistress**, Anne Boleyn, who was his wife's **lady-in-waiting**. She was the second of six wives in total – two he divorced, two he **beheaded** and one died a natural death.

Henry is also remembered for the English Reformation. He **dissolved monasteries**, taking their land and treasures for the state. This was the start of a long and bitter religious divide in Britain. In the decades that followed, thousands of Catholics and Protestants were **tortured** and executed because of their religious beliefs.

The golden age

Elizabeth I, the last Tudor monarch, was the daughter of Henry VIII and Anne Boleyn. Her 45 years on the throne from 1558 to 1603 are often referred to as the "golden age" in British history. Elizabethan England produced the **playwrights** William Shakespeare and Christopher Marlowe as well as musicians like William Byrd and Thomas Tallis. Francis Bacon developed the scientific method, which became a central element of the **Enlightenment**. Men on ships went out to explore new continents, and Sir Francis Drake became the first Brit to sail around the world in 1580. Eight years later, the same man led the British fleet against the Spanish Armada when King Philip II of Spain attempted to invade Britain.

Elizabeth was a popular and charismatic monarch. The "**Virgin** Queen" never married, claiming she **was devoted** only **to** her country. She had moderate religious views and allowed different beliefs, as long as these remained private. However, several Catholic **plots** threatened her life. One of these was linked to her cousin Mary Stuart, Queen of Scots, who Elizabeth finally had executed after 19 years in jail.

Bonfire Night
When the Gunpowder Plot was discovered, Londoners lit bonfires to give thanks. The British still celebrate this event with bonfires and fireworks on 5 November each year. Don't worry if you see a man tied to a chair in the flames – it's only clothes stuffed with paper. It's traditional to "burn the Guy"!

The Gunpowder Plot

The plots continued after Elizabeth's death, when the English throne went to Mary Stuart's Protestant son James, who had been King of Scotland since he was a baby. In 1605, a group of Catholic **conspirators** rented a cellar next to the Houses of Parliament. They hid 36 barrels of gunpowder underground and prepared to blow up King James and his government on 5 November. Fortunately, the plot was discovered by spies and stopped just in time. One of the **traitors**, Guy Fawkes, was caught and tortured for two days until he revealed the secrets of his group.

determined	entschlossen
heir	Erbe
mistress	Geliebte
lady-in-waiting	Kammerfrau
to behead	enthaupten
to dissolve	auflösen
monastery	Kloster
to torture	foltern
playwright	Dramatiker(in)
Enlightenment	Aufklärung
virgin	Jungfrau
to be devoted to	treu ergeben sein
plot	Verschwörung
gunpowder	Schießpulver
bonfire	Freudenfeuer, Lagerfeuer
conspirator	Verschwörer(in)
traitor	Verräter(in)

1 The Wars of the Roses. Unterstreichen Sie die sechs Grammatikfehler im Text und korrigieren Sie sie!

The Wars of the Roses were fighted between the House of York and the House of Lancaster, each of which sometimes used a rose as a emblem. Both royal houses have wanted the English throne, what resulted in a long civil war that lasted from 1455 to 1485. The conflict ended when Henry Tudor, a Welshman of who his mother was from the House of Lancaster, defeated Richard III from the House of York at the Battle of Bosworth. He became King Henry VII and married Elizabeth of York, that united the two houses. The Tudor rose, which remained the symbol of the Tudor dynasty, combined the red Lancaster rose with the white York rose.

The Tudor rose

1. .... 2. ....

3. .... 4. ....

5. .... 6. ....

2 History quiz. Testen Sie Ihr Geschichtswissen!

1. ☐ This king married his first wife when he was only 11 years old.
2. ☐ This playwright was possibly a spy for Elizabeth I.
3. ☐ This English king was beheaded in 1649.
4. ☐ This man replaced the king and called himself “Lord Protector” after the English Civil War (1642 to 1651).
5. ☐ In 1688, the English replaced a Catholic king with this Protestant.
6. ☐ The main English translation of the Bible is named after this king.

a) William of Orange
b) Oliver Cromwell
c) Henry VIII
d) James I
e) Christopher Marlowe
f) Charles I

3 Good Queen Bess. Ordnen Sie die hervorgehobenen Begriffe in der Rede der Queen vor dem Kampf gegen die Amada ihren Bedeutungen zu!

Elizabeth I as defeater of the Armada, showing her international power

My loving people, let tyrants fear! I have always so behaved myself that, under God, I have placed my **chiefest** strength in the loyal hearts and goodwill of my subjects; and therefore I am come amongst you, as you see, at this time, not for my recreation and **disport**, but being **resolved**, in the **midst** and heat of the battle, to live and die amongst you all; to lay down for my God, and for my kingdom, and my people, my honour and my blood, even in the dust.
I know I have the body of a weak, **feeble** woman; but I have the heart and stomach of a king, and of a king of England too, and think **foul scorn** that Parma or Spain, or any prince of Europe, should dare to invade the borders of my **realm**; to which rather than any dishonour shall grow by me, I myself will take up **arms**, I myself will be your general, judge, and rewarder of every one of your virtues in the field.

1. middle	....	2. decided	....
3. powerless	....	4. kingdom	....
5. weapons	....	6. greatest	....
7. amusement	....	8. no respect	....

4 Odd one out. Welches Wort ist das „schwarze Schaf"? Unterstreichen Sie!

1. **traitor conspiracy treason tyrant**
2. **Vatican Reformation monastery Catholic**
3. **Byrd Tallis Fawkes Bacon**
4. **January bonfire fireworks November**
5. **suspicious devoted pious religious**
6. **torture behead execute devote**

Uniting the nations

Have you ever wondered how Britain was able to create the largest **empire** the world has ever seen? The story begins with the birth of the United Kingdom.
England became a united nation in the 10th century and took control of Wales in 1284 under Edward I. To symbolize his power, the English king made his son Prince of Wales – a title that is still used for the British **heir to the throne**.
Scotland was an independent nation for several centuries. When Elizabeth I died without an heir in 1603, King James VI of Scotland became King of England, too. Even though the two countries now shared a monarch, they remained separate states until 1707, when Scotland decided to **join** the United Kingdom.
English rule in Ireland began in the 12th century. In 1536, Henry VIII named himself King of Ireland and many non-Irish **nobles** were given land and power in the years that followed, especially in the north. Ireland finally joined the United Kingdom in 1801, but it was not a happy marriage. In 1922, after years of conflict and fighting, the south broke away from the union, while the north decided to remain in the UK.

The British Empire

At its height, the British Empire was the largest empire in history. In the late 16th century, Sir Francis Drake sailed all the way around the globe, and England began to establish colonies and **trade** in the Americas and Asia. In the 17th and 18th centuries, the search for wealth and power overseas continued, which also resulted in a series of wars with other European colonial powers.

By 1783, Britain had taken control of India and Canada, but it had also lost its 13 American colonies in the American War of Independence. About this time, parts of Australia and New Zealand were added to the Empire. Australia was initially a **penal colony**, and criminals from

Britain were sent "down under" to **populate** the enormous continent. In the 19th century, the Empire expanded further, and Britain became the world's dominant colonial power. By 1921, a fifth of the world's population and nearly a quarter of the Earth's total land area belonged to the British Empire. People were right to say that "the sun never sets on the British Empire!"

The song "Rule, Britannia!" dates back to the mid-18th century and reflects the nation's sense of power and confidence at that time: "Rule, Britannia! Britannia, rule the waves. Britons never shall be slaves." Today the piece is always played at the Last Night of the Proms to a crowd of people waving the Union Jack.

The Victorian age (1837-1901)

Under Queen Victoria, Britain was without doubt the world's most powerful nation. Between 1805 and the First World War, the **Royal Navy** was not **challenged**. It was a period of relative peace in Europe, and the Victorians believed that such harmony was necessary for long-term **prosperity**.

Global trade was already booming when Victoria came to the throne. Britain, home to the Industrial Revolution, exported textiles, metals and innovative technology all over the world. **Steamships** made it even easier to transport sugar, tobacco and cotton from the Caribbean as well as tea, **silk** and **spices** from India. At the same time, the railway radically changed how people could travel, communicate and do business. And thousands of miles of cable at the bottom of the sea made it possible to send a telegraph to almost every part of the Empire.

empire	Imperium	**to populate**	bevölkern
heir to the throne	Erbprinz, Erbprinzessin	**Royal Navy**	Königliche Marine
to join	sich anschließen, Mitglied werden	**to challenge**	herausfordern
		prosperity	Wohlstand
noble	Adlige(r)	**steamship**	Dampfer
trade	Handel	**silk**	Seide
penal colony	Strafkolonie	**spices** *pl*	Gewürze

1 Britain and the Empire. Welche Antwort ist richtig? Kreuzen Sie an!

1. Scotland established a colony in 1698. It failed because of malaria and attacks by the Spanish, and Scotland lost a quarter of all its capital. Where was this colony?
   a) ❑ The Gold Coast b) ❑ Canada c) ❑ Panama

2. Because of their history, one stereotype about Australians is that they are all … .
   a) ❑ criminals b) ❑ lazy c) ❑ stupid

3. The Empire faced a large rebellion in 1857 when a local army shot their British officers and marched on the capital. Where was this?
   a) ❑ Ireland b) ❑ India c) ❑ America

4. What percentage of the world's population lived in the British Empire in 1901?
   a) ❑ 10% b) ❑ 25% c) ❑ 33%

5. The first permanent English settlement in America was called … .
   a) ❑ Jamestown b) ❑ New Plymouth c) ❑ Cuper's Cove

2 Famous Victorians. Warum sind diese Menschen gut bekannt? Ordnen Sie zu!

1. ☐ Florence Nightingale
2. ☐ Isambard Kingdom Brunel
3. ☐ John Cadbury
4. ☐ Jack the Ripper
5. ☐ Charles Dickens
6. ☐ Elizabeth Fry

a) A popular author who also went on tour to read dramatic passages from his books.
b) A social reformer who helped poor families as well as women and children in prisons.
c) A serial killer who murdered prostitutes in London's East End.
d) A founder of modern nursing who helped many soldiers and improved hospitals.
e) A brilliant engineer who designed bridges, railways, trains and steamships.
f) A chocolate factory owner from Birmingham who developed the chocolate bar.

3 The Great Exhibition. Vervollständigen Sie den Text mit den fehlenden Wörtern!

building aim catalogue exhibits ceremony event technology

The Great Exhibition (Weltausstellung) of 1851 was a high point for British culture in the Victorian period. It was the first international 1. .... of its kind and took place at the amazing Crystal Palace in London's Hyde Park. There were around 100,000 things to look at from all over the world. Half of the 2. .... were products and inventions from the United Kingdom. The 3. .... was to show the world and the British public how great the country was at design, 4. .... and art. There were also rooms for exotic items from other nations – including a dead Indian elephant!
The exhibition was organized by Prince Albert, the German-born husband of Queen Victoria, and the royal couple were at the opening 5. .... on 1 May. At the start, tickets were only for the rich upper classes: gentlemen paid £3 and ladies £2. Later, the working classes paid much less to enter. In total, around 6 million people visited the great glass 6. .... designed by Joseph Paxton. Albert used the profits to build museums, and you can see his statue outside the Royal Albert Hall, where he is holding a copy of the exhibition 7. ....

4 Countries in the Empire. Welche Länder des Empire sind im Buchstabenchaos versteckt?

1. i o n g r a p e s ....
2. s t o h u f a r a c i S ....
3. l i a r s a a u t ....
4. m a a j a c i ....
5. w n e z a l e n a d ....
6. i r r e s a o n l e e S ....
7. a r m b u ....
8. y e n a k ....

The mother of democracy

The United Kingdom is a monarchy with a long parliamentary tradition and is sometimes called "the mother of democracy". You will find versions of Britain's political system all over the world, especially in countries that were once part of the Empire. And yet Britain is one of only four countries in the world with no written **constitution**! How is that possible? The **law of the land** is based on a collection of documents and agreements, so the British constitution is always changing. It is a little different every time Parliament reforms a law.

Order in the house!

Parliament meets in the Palace of Westminster. There are two houses: the House of Commons and the House of Lords. There is a **general election** at least every five years and the leader of the winning party becomes the prime minister. The country has 650 **constituencies**, and the candidate with the most **votes** in each constituency becomes a **Member of Parliament** (MP) in the House of Commons. This is called the **"first past the post" system**. It means that the percentage of votes for each party is not really important. For example, in 2010 the third largest party took 23% of the votes but won only around 11% of the seats.

The House of Lords is **independent** from the House of Commons. Its role is to check and **challenge** the work of government, and it often asks for changes to **draft laws**. There were over 780 members ("peers") in 2014, but this number is not fixed. The Queen **appoints** new lords and ladies that the prime minister suggests, and they keep this title for life. Many peers were once MPs, but there are also leading names in business as well as important cultural and religious figures.

The prime minister lives here

Leading the way

There are some political leaders you simply cannot forget. Margaret Thatcher (Conservative, 1979–90) and Tony Blair (Labour, 1997–2007) both changed the image of Britain when they were prime minister. Thatcher was Britain's first woman prime minister. She made many unpopular decisions such as closing **mines**, ignoring the protests of **trade unions** and stopping free milk in schools (she was called "Thatcher the **milk snatcher**"). However, the "Iron Lady" also won the Falklands War and successfully fought against Brussels a lot. Her decision to privatize **public services** still **divides** the nation.

Blair came to power with a **landslide victory** and gave the country new optimism at the start of the millennium. He placed many women in important positions ("Blair's Babes"), created regional parliaments in Wales, Scotland and Northern Ireland and was a charismatic speaker. However, after **9/11** he also led Britain into a very **controversial** war in Iraq. The Labour government also broke many promises, for example by making students pay more for university. Blair was therefore sometimes known as "B-**Liar**" in the press.

constitution	Verfassung	**draft law**	Gesetzesentwurf
law of the land	geltendes Recht	**to appoint**	ernennen
general election	Unterhauswahlen	**mine**	Bergwerk
constituency	Wahlkreis	**trade union**	Gewerkschaft
vote	Stimme; Abstimmung	**〰 milk snatcher**	Milchdieb(in)
Member of Parliament (MP)	Abgeordnete(r)	**public services** *pl*	öffentliche Dienstleitungen
"first past the post" system	Mehrheitswahlsystem	**to divide**	spalten
		landslide victory	Erdrutschsieg
independent	unabhängig	**9/11**	der 11. September
to challenge	herausfordern, in Frage stellen	**controversial**	umstritten
		liar	Lügner(in)

1 True or false? Welche Aussagen sind korrekt? Kreuzen Sie an!

1. The United Kingdom does not have a constitution. ❑
2. A general election takes place every five years. ❑
3. If a party wins enough seats, it can win an election even if most people in the country didn't vote for that party. ❑
4. There were only two coalitions in the UK between 1945 and 2015. ❑
5. Blair was a popular prime minister when he left office in 2007. ❑
6. Thatcher was a strong leader but also a very controversial one. ❑
7. The UK has a "special relationship" with the United States. ❑

2 Winston Churchill. Ergänzen Sie den Text bei Bedarf mit den fehlenden Artikeln!

Winston Churchill is one of 1. .... greatest figures in 2. .... British history. He was born into a rich family in 1874 and began life as 3. .... soldier and part-time journalist. He became 4. .... MP in 1900, first as a Conservative and then as a Liberal. After leading the Royal Navy in World War I, he left the Liberals to join the Conservative Party again, and he managed 5. .... country's finances until 1929. In 1940, Parliament chose Churchill to be prime minister of an all-party coalition government. The country was already at 6. .... war. Churchill had a wonderfully strong personality and he was 7. .... great statesman. His unforgettable speeches motivated the nation and united 8. .... country in its "Darkest Hour". Surprisingly, he then lost the general election in 1945. He became prime minister again in 1951, but he was old and unwell. At times he had to work from 9. .... bed! He resigned after four years and received 10. .... state funeral in 1965.

3 Laws and civil rights. Wann fanden diese historischen Entwicklungen in Großbritannien statt? Ordnen Sie zu!

1. ☐ 1215
2. ☐ 1833
3. ☐ 1857
4. ☐ 1906
5. ☐ 1918
6. ☐ 1928
7. ☐ 1964
8. ☐ 1967

a) All men over 21 and all women over 30 can vote.
b) The death penalty is used for the last time.
c) Divorce becomes possible for everyone in the Victorian age.
d) It is legal for women in England, Wales and Scotland to end a pregnancy.
e) Workers in trade unions are able to go on strike.
f) A document called the Magna Carta limits the power of the king.
g) All women over 21 can vote.
h) Slavery is made illegal throughout the British Empire.

4 Unusual laws. Ergänzen Sie die Sätze mit den fehlenden Wörtern und entdecken Sie einige seltsame Gesetze aus Großbritannien!

jump drunk pet play

1. It is illegal to be .... in a pub.
2. You may not let your .... have sex with a royal dog.
3. It is illegal to .... the queue when buying a Tube ticket.
4. It is illegal to .... in the snow on the street.

5 Did you know? Kennen Sie die richtige Antwort? Kreuzen Sie an!

1. The prime minister lives at this famous address.
   a) ☐ 10 Downing Street b) ☐ 50 Baker Street c) ☐ 1 Piccadilly Circus

2. This person signs all new laws to make them official.
   a) ☐ the prime minister b) ☐ the monarch c) ☐ the lord chancellor

3. This part of Parliament is sometimes called “the Upper House”.
   a) ☐ the Cabinet b) ☐ the House of Commons c) ☐ the House of Lords

From Empire to Commonwealth

What is Britain's place in the global community in the twenty-first century? Instead of being the centre of the British Empire, the UK is a member of the Commonwealth of Nations – a union of more than 50 **independent** countries that were once part of the British Empire. Here **diversity** and friendly cooperation are more important than power and trade. On the whole, most Brits accept the fact that their country is no longer a global superpower. They are generally **proud** of their past, and you will see examples of patriotism everywhere. At the same time, people from the UK often distance themselves from the rest of Europe.

An outsider in Europe?

The British have been debating whether to be in or out of Europe since the 1950s. Back in 1973, two-thirds of all Brits supported the decision to join the **European Economic Community**, as the European Union was then called. Later, however, many turned against the idea of a European Parliament. Especially unpopular was the movement towards greater European integration and a **single currency** that began in the 1980s. Eurosceptics said that the European Union had become too powerful and that it reduced national **sovereignty**. From the 1990s onwards and especially because of the euro crisis, their **influence** was growing. In the 2014 European elections, anti-European party UKIP won 28% of the **votes** – more than any of its rivals. A referendum on whether or not the country should stay in the EU took place in June 2016 – and 52% voted for leaving. This started the so-called "Brexit" process.

The British pound

The pound sterling is the oldest currency that is still **in circulation**. It first appeared in the eighth century, back when Britain as we know it today did not exist. The value of a pound was originally a pound in **weight** ("libra pondo") of sterling silver, which explains why the pound sign (£) is based on the letter "L". It is traditional for the monarch to appear on one side of all coins and notes. Queen Elizabeth II holds the world record for appearing on the most currencies because her portrait is also found around the Commonwealth. The Bank of England also puts great British figures like Dickens and Darwin on the back of its notes.

> Banks in Scotland and Northern Ireland print their own notes. These sometimes look very different to the money printed by the Bank of England! But don't worry - you can use any pound banknote anywhere in the UK.

Immigration into Britain

In the 1950s, there was a huge wave of immigration from the Commonwealth, which was welcomed due to a **shortage of workers**. The cultures that these immigrants from former colonies brought with them have influenced British life significantly, especially the Indian, Pakistani and Afro-Caribbean cultures. You can find Asian food almost everywhere, and multicultural Britain has become an **established** part of daily life, appearing in music, literature and film.

Today, most new immigrants come from India, the European Union and Australia. And with this new wave of immigration, the **social make-up** of Britain continues to change. For example, the 2011 **census** showed that Polish is now the second language in England with 546,000 speakers (about 1%) – practically the same number as for Welsh in all of Britain!

Notting Hill Carnival

independent	unabhängig	**vote**	Stimme; Abstimmung
diversity	Vielfalt	**in circulation**	im Umlauf
proud	stolz	**weight**	Gewicht
European Economic Community	Europäische Wirtschaftsgemeinschaft	**shortage of workers**	Arbeitskräftemangel
single currency	Einheitswährung	**established**	anerkannt, akzeptiert
sovereignty	Souveränität	**social make-up**	soziale Struktur
influence	Einfluss	**census**	Volkszählung

1 The Commonwealth. Welche Antwort ist richtig? Kreuzen Sie an!

1. The Commonwealth of Nations covers every continent and almost a quarter of the world's land area. Approximately how many people live in these countries?
   a) ❑ 1.3 billion b) ❑ 2.3 billion c) ❑ 3.3 billion

2. What is the relationship between the member states of the Commonwealth?
   a) ❑ It is a hierarchy under Britain. b) ❑ They have to be loyal to Britain. c) ❑ They are free and equal.

3. What do all countries in the Commonwealth have in common besides their history and culture?
   a) ❑ the English language b) ❑ the pound sterling as a currency c) ❑ the same head of state

4. How frequently do the Commonwealth Games take place?
   a) ❑ every year b) ❑ every 4 years c) ❑ every 5 years

5. The first Commonwealth Games, originally called the British Empire Games, took place in Hamilton, Canada, in which year?
   a) ❑ 1851 b) ❑ 1947 c) ❑ 1930

6. Which of the following Commonwealth countries does not have Queen Elizabeth II as its sovereign but its own monarch as Head of State?
   a) ❑ Malaysia b) ❑ Barbados c) ❑ Papua New Guinea

Welcome to Britain!

Exercise 1: **1.** b **2.** a **3.** c **4.** a

Exercise 2: **1.** sevententh (seventeenth) **2.** Gravity (gravity) **3.** their (there) **4.** english (English) **5.** rote (wrote) **6.** populer (popular)

Exercise 3:

1 P						2 G		
O			3 S		4 L	E	F	5 T
U			T			O		E
N			O			R		A
6 D	O	W	N	I	N	G		T
			E			E		I
7 B	L	E	S	S				M
					8 M	I	L	E

Exercise 4: **1.** Birmingham **2.** Severn **3.** Thames

London's calling

Exercise 1: **1.** enjoy **2.** take **3.** talk **4.** spoken **5.** turn **6.** say

Exercise 2: **1.** history **2.** century **3.** cathedral **4.** view **5.** palace **6.** attraction **7.** growth **8.** landmark **Hidden word:** Hyde Park

Exercise 3: **1.** Wimbledon **2.** The Tower of London **3.** The Tube **4.** The British Museum **5.** The Square Mile **6.** Samuel Johnson

Exercise 4: **1.** multiculturalest (most multicultural) **2.** are born (were born) **3.** less than half is (less than half are) **4.** are hearing (will/can hear) **5.** it gives (there are) **6.** on the world (in the world)

Merry England

Exercise 1: **1.** f, stream **2.** c, mountain **3.** a, stone wall **4.** g, hedge **5.** b, forest **6.** d, field **7.** e, river

Exercise 2: **1.** said **2.** are **3.** sell **4.** live **5.** exists **6.** survive

Exercise 3: **1.** city **2.** grim **3.** mining **4.** rich

Exercise 4: **1.** An Englishman invented the World Wide Web.
2. French was the official language in England for 300 years.
3. The world's first stamp appeared in England in 1840.
4. Beef is one of England's biggest exports.

Exercise 5: **1.** e **2.** d **3.** a **4.** g **5.** f **6.** b **7.** c

The Welsh dragon

Exercise 1: **1.** a **2.** a **3.** c **4.** b

Exercise 2: **1.** blindly **2.** possible **3.** well **4.** fluent **5.** famously

Exercise 3:

1 A							
C					2 B		
R		3 B		4 N	E	X	5 T
6 O	V	E	R		T		H
S		H			W		R
S		I			E		O
		N			E		U
		7 D	O	W	N		G
							H

Exercise 4: **1.** true **2.** true **3.** false – Cardiff Castle is one of many sights. **4.** false – Children have to learn Welsh until they are 16. **5.** true **6.** false – The south coast has the densest population.

Bonnie Scotland

Exercise 1: **1.** Hadrian's Wall was built by the Romans to protect themselves from the "barbarians" in the north.

2. The popular Hadrian's Wall footpath can be followed for 135 km.

3. You will be taken (by the path) through some beautiful, wild and remote countryside.

4. Hadrian's Wall was made a World Heritage Site (by UNESCO) in 1987.

Exercise 2: **1.** e **2.** a **3.** d **4.** c **5.** b

Exercise 3: **1.** village **2.** border **3.** popular **4.** weddings **5.** home **6.** reason **7.** Nowadays **8.** apart from/except (for)

Exercise 4: **1.** d **2.** f **3.** e **4.** a **5.** c **6.** b **7.** h **8.** g

The Ireland less known

Exercise 1: **1.** tensions **2.** headline **3.** giant **4.** economic **5.** minority **6.** hospitality **7.** civil rights **8.** rock formation **Hidden word:** shamrock

Exercise 2: **1.** e **2.** a **3.** f **4.** b **5.** d **6.** c

Meet the royals

Exercise 1: **1.** false – They are British, although some of their ancestors were foreign. **2.** true **3.** true **4.** true **5.** false – About three-quarters of Brits support the monarchy. **6.** true **7.** true

Exercise 2: **1.** Sandringham House **2.** The Palace of Holyrood-house **3.** Windsor Castle **4.** The Tower of London **5.** Buckingham Palace **6.** Balmoral Castle

Exercise 3: **1.** are **2.** already **3.** redesigned **4.** its own **5.** some of

Exercise 4:

		1 W								2 R
3 H	E	A	D	O	F	S	T	4 A	T	E
		L						B		P
5 D	U	K	E					R		U
		A				6 R		O		B
7 J	U	B	I	8 L	E	E		A		L
		O		I		I		D		I
		U		O		G				C
		T		N		N				

Show some class!

Exercise 1: **1.** b **2.** f **3.** d **4.** e **5.** a **6.** c

Exercise 2: **1.** f **2.** e **3.** d **4.** a **5.** b **6.** c

Exercise 3: **1.** The word "snob" has been adopted by almost every European language.
2. Geoffrey is teased (by them) about eating fast food.
3. He is judged (by people) because of his strong Liverpool accent.
4. Social status is defined by family background, education and accent.
5. An old banger was parked in my mother's front garden by some chavs.
6. The palace and its land are being bought by a business tycoon.

Exercise 4: **1.** class system **2.** aristocrats **3.** celebrities **4.** toffs **5.** snob **6.** chavs **7.** stereotype

British humour

Exercise 1: **1.** e **2.** a **3.** b **4.** d **5.** f **6.** c

Exercise 2: **1.** rain (reign) **2.** Nappy (Happy) **3.** wurst (worst) **4.** chew (you) **5.** toupee (to pay) **6.** sand (hand) **7.** busyness (business) **8.** shelf (self)

Exercise 3: **1.** c **2.** d **3.** b **4.** e **5.** a

Exercise 4: **1.** The land of embarrassment and breakfast.
2. They are the only people who like to be told how bad things are.
3. You cannot trust people who have such bad cuisine.
4. England and America are two countries separated by the same language.
5. Class is the British language.
6. They do not want to be happy; they want to be right.

Eating British

Exercise 1: **1.** order **2.** bar **3.** barmaid **4.** round **5.** tip **6.** served **7.** waitress

Exercise 2: **1.** a **2.** d **3.** h **4.** g **5.** f **6.** c **7.** b **8.** e

Exercise 3: **1.** Lancashire hotpot **2.** Cornish pasty **3.** Cumberland sausage **4.** scone **5.** Yorkshire pudding **6.** chicken tikka masala

Exercise 4: **1.** c **2.** b **3.** a **4.** a **5.** b **6.** a **7.** c

Mad about sport

Exercise 1: **1.** rugby **2.** snooker **3.** badminton **4.** football

Exercise 2: **1.** f **2.** e **3.** b **4.** c **5.** g **6.** a **7.** d

Literature

Exercise 1: **1.** Hamlet **2.** Richard III **3.** Juliet **4.** Mark Anthony **5.** Shylock **6.** Lady Macbeth

Exercise 2: **1.** Many masterpieces of literature (literary masterpieces) have been adapted for cinema and television.
2. Miss Marple is a popular character by Agatha Christie who likes to help the police.
3. We know surprisingly little about Shakespeare and his private life.
4. Dickens was incredibly successful in the Victorian era (in Victorian times).
5. In total, Doyle wrote 56 stories and four novels about Holmes.

Exercise 3: **1.** e **2.** f **3.** c **4.** a **5.** d **6.** b

Exercise 4: **1.** by **2.** from **3.** After **4.** in/during **5.** to **6.** of **7.** by **8.** into

Exercise 5: **1.** e **2.** c **3.** f **4.** a **5.** g **6.** d **7.** b

The sound of music

Exercise 1: **1.** both **2.** used to **3.** along **4.** outfits **5.** more excited **6.** broke up

Exercise 2: **1.** c, classical **2.** d, heavy metal **3.** g, punk rock **4.** e, Britpop **5.** a, pop **6.** h, soul **7.** b, ska **8.** f, rock

Exercise 3: **1.** begun (began) **2.** most great (greatest) **3.** every where (everywhere) **4.** selled (sold) **5.** then (than) **6.** sucessful (successful)

Exercise 4:

		1 C					2 F			3 A
	4 C	O	M	5 P	O	S	E	R		N
		N		R			S			T
		D		O			T			H
		U		M			I			E
		C		S			V			M
		T			6 C	H	A	R	T	S
		O					L			
7 K	A	R	A	O	K	E				

Stage and screen

Exercise 1: **1.** audience **2.** miners **3.** instalment **4.** programme **5.** soap

Hidden word: cinema

Exercise 2: **1.** watched **2.** has produced **3.** have seen **4.** played **5.** paid **6.** was

Exercise 3: **1.** true **2.** true **3.** false – The *Carry On* series has the most instalments. **4.** false – Sean Connery was the first Bond. **5.** true **6.** false – Around half of all ticket sales are in London. **7.** true **8.** true

Exercise 4: **1.** f **2.** e **3.** a **4.** b **5.** c **6.** d

Exercise 5: **1.** b **2.** a **3.** c **4.** c

Art and design

Exercise 1: **1.** walk **2.** collections **3.** human **4.** established/founded **5.** centuries

Exercise 2:

1 C	2 O	3 N	4 T	5 E	6 M	7 P
22 M	23 I	24 N	25 O	26 U	27 V	8 O
21 E	36 L	37 L	38 U	39 C	28 E	9 R
20 V	35 U	42 N	41 A	40 I	29 A	10 A
19 O	34 K	33 S	32 N	31 R	30 U	11 R
18 D	17 O	16 G	15 N	14 U	13 O	12 Y

Britain's early history

Exercise 1: **1.** have inhabited **2.** used **3.** AD **4.** counties **5.** conquerors **6.** eye **7.** property **8.** Norman **9.** French

Exercise 2: **1.** monarch/ruler **2.** kingdoms **3.** Vikings **4.** invaders/attackers **5.** settlements **6.** Latin **7.** describe

Exercise 3: **1.** c **2.** c **3.** b **4.** b **5.** c **6.** a

Exercise 4: **1.** tribe **2.** unique **3.** violence **4.** raid **5.** tapestry **Hidden word:** invade

Tudor kings and queens

Exercise 1: **1.** fighted (fought) **2.** a emblem (an emblem) **3.** have wanted (wanted) **4.** what resulted (which resulted) **5.** of who his mother (whose mother) **6.** that united (uniting/which united)

Exercise 2: **1.** c **2.** e **3.** f **4.** b **5.** a **6.** d

Exercise 3: **1.** midst **2.** resolved **3.** feeble **4.** realm **5.** arms **6.** chiefest **7.** disport **8.** foul scorn

Exercise 4: **1.** tyrant **2.** Reformation **3.** Fawkes **4.** January **5.** suspicious **6.** devote

Rule, Britannia!

Exercise 1: **1.** c **2.** a **3.** b **4.** b **5.** a

Exercise 2: **1.** d **2.** e **3.** f **4.** c **5.** a **6.** b

Exercise 3: **1.** event **2.** exhibits **3.** aim **4.** technology **5.** ceremony **6.** building **7.** catalogue

Exercise 4: **1.** Singapore **2.** South Africa **3.** Australia **4.** Jamaica **5.** New Zealand **6.** Sierra Leone **7.** Burma **8.** Kenya

The mother of democracy

Exercise 1: **1.** false – The constitution is not written down in one document. **2.** false – It takes place at least every five years (sometimes less). **3.** true **4.** true **5.** false – The war in Iraq made him unpopular, and some say he was a liar. **6.** true **7.** true

Exercise 2: **1.** the **2.** – **3.** a **4.** an **5.** the **6.** – **7.** a **8.** the **9.** – **10.** a

Exercise 3: **1.** f **2.** h **3.** c **4.** e **5.** a **6.** g **7.** b **8.** d

Exercise 4: **1.** drunk **2.** pet **3.** jump **4.** play

Exercise 5: **1.** a **2.** b **3.** c

Britain today

Exercise 1: **1.** b **2.** c **3.** a **4.** b **5.** c **6.** a

Bildnachweis
123rf: Kanstantsin Prymachuk 7 (unten), 8 (oben), 14 (oben), 18 (oben), 22 (oben), 26 (oben); Georgios Kollidas 8 (zweites v. o.); Matt Trommer 18 (unten); Anthony Brindley 20 (links); Jacek Nowak 23; speedfighter 29 (Mitte), 87; eyewave 38 (oben); SUNG KUK KIM 44; Anthony Baggett 55; lightwise 60; V. J. Matthew 65 (Mitte), 80; claudiodivizia 66 (links); stocksolutions 66 (unten); armvector 72; David Fowler 79 (oben); jonybigude 82 (oben)
flickr: Sue Hasker 32 (oben links); Valdiney Pimenta (unten Mitte); Piotr Drabik 36 (Nr. 4)
fotolia: John Gomez 4 (zweites v. o.), 29 (rechts unten), 34 (oben); peresanz 18 (Mitte); BasPhoto 32 (oben rechts); snaptitude 49 (Mitte), 52; jorisvo 67, 69; sborisov 78 (links)
iStockphoto: sborisov 5 (rechts), 10 (oben); BreatheFitness 12 (oben); EdStock2 39; whitemay 41; saintho 46; isitsharp 47 (oben); Gannet77 47 (unten); EdStock 59 (unten), 79 (unten); flutophilus 66 (oben); chrisdorney 78 (unten); justhavealook 84
picture alliance: empics 4 (unten), 30 (unten); Everett Collection 29 (links), 38 (unten); dpa – Report 35; United Archives/IFTN 51; CPA Media 73
pixabay: FrankWinkler 5 (Mitte), 6 (unten), 22 (unten); Elektro-Plan 7 (oben); WikiImages 8 (unten links), 65 (oben), 70 (unten); stevebidmead 8 (drittes v. o.); skeeze 8 (unten rechts); scharfsascha 10 (links); Witizia 12 (unten); PublicDomainPictures 15 (unten); contagiousbasti 16; juliaavisphillips 20 (rechts); MemoryCatcher 32 (unten rechts); falco 43 (oben), jackmac34 43 (unten); Unsplash 56/57 (Hintergrund); hurk 64; stux 82 (unten)
privat: Helga Aichele 26 (links, unten), 27
shutterstock: Robert Biedermann 3, 5 (oben); jaroslava V 4 (oben), 5 (links); okili77 6 (oben); Arena Photo UK 9; Mapics 10 (unten); Andrei Nekrassov 15 (oben); Len Green 19; ronfromyork 25; Martin Lisner 29 (oben); Dutourdumonde Photography 30 (oben); Phil Jones 31; Brendan Howard 32 (oben Mitte); Joe Seer 34 (links), 36 (rechts); Featureflash 36 (Nr. 1, 2, 5); Debu55y 42 (oben); Bratwustle 42 (unten); Birsen Cebeci 58, 89; Ron Ellis 62 (unten); Stephen Clarke 63; Paul Cummings 75; Bikeworldtravel 83
wikipedia: Library of Congress: cph 3c11094 4 (drittes v. o.), 54; Bob Collowan 11, 32 (unten links); Dr Greg based on Nilfanion 14; Library of Congress: var.0742 22 (Mitte); www.number10.gov.uk 36 (Nr. 3); Martin Droeshout, Beinecke Rare Book & Manuscript Library, Yale University 49 (oben), 50 (oben); National Portrait Gallery, London: NPG3630 50 (unten); Cyotethndr 53; www.flickr.com/people/emutree 54 (unten); Monika Rittershaus, Pressestelle der Stiftung Berliner Philharmoniker 57; www.flickr.com/photos/bellaphon 59 (oben); John Constable, The Yorck Project 62 (oben); William Turner, The Yorck Project 49 (unten), 62 (Mitte); Workshop of Hans Holbein the Younger, Walker Art Gallery: WAG 1350 70 (oben); National Portrait Gallery, London: NPG 109 71; Walter Crane, maps.bpl.org/id/M8682 65 (unten links), 74

pl	Plural
sth.	something
↯	umgangssprachlich

A

accessible	zugänglich
alive and kicking	höchst lebendig
ancient	antik, uralt
anthem	*hier:* Kracher, Hymne
antidote	*hier:* Gegenmittel
to appear	erscheinen
to appoint	ernennen
art nouveau	Jugendstil
the arts *pl*	*hier:* Kunst und Kultur
attack	Angriff, Überfall
attraction	*hier:* Sehenswürdigkeit
audience	Publikum, Zuschauer
to avoid	vermeiden

B

bagpipes *pl*	Dudelsack
↯ bangers and mash	Bratwürste mit Kartoffelbrei
banter	Wortgeplänkel
battered	im Rührteig frittiert
to be actively involved in	sich aktiv einbringen in, sich engagieren
to be devoted to	treu ergeben sein
to be fluent in …	… fließend sprechen
to behead	enthaupten
to be made up of	bestehen aus
bold	gewagt
bonfire	Freudenfeuer, Lagerfeuer
bonnie *Scottish*	hübsch, schön
borough	Stadtbezirk
bowler hat	Melone
break-up	Trennung, Auflösung
↯ brew	eine Tasse Tee, *wörtl.* Gebräu
broadcasting company	Rundfunkgesellschaft

C

to carry on	weitermachen
census	Volkszählung
challenge	Herausforderung
to challenge	herausfordern, in Frage stellen
chapter	Kapitel
charitable	wohltätig, gemeinnützig
↯ chav	Proll
civil rights *pl*	Bürgerrechte
class divide	Klassenunterschiede
common	*hier:* gemeinsam
composer	Komponist(in)
conductor	Dirigent(in)
conquest	Eroberung
conspirator	Verschwörer(in)
constituency	Wahlkreis
constitution	Verfassung
contemporary	zeitgenössisch
controversial	umstritten
converted	umgebaut
county	Grafschaft
Crown Jewels *pl*	Kronjuwelen
cultural heritage	Kulturerbe

D

daffodil	Narzisse
to date back to	stammen aus
day trip	Tagesausflug
decade	Jahrzehnt
to defeat	besiegen, schlagen
to delight	erfreuen, entzücken
determined	entschlossen
Diamond Jubilee	60. Thronjubiläum
to display	zeigen, ausstellen
to dissolve	auflösen
distinctive	charakteristisch
disturbing	verstörend
diverse	vielfältig
diversity	Vielfalt
to divide	spalten
divided up	aufgeteilt in
divine right	göttliches Recht
division	Spaltung, Trennung
doom and gloom	Pessimismus, Untergangsstimmung
dove	weiße Taube
draft law	Gesetzesentwurf
dragon	Drache
duke, duchess	Herzog, Herzogin

E

eclectic	bunt gemischt
economic	wirtschaftlich
economic centre	Wirtschaftszentrum
economic opportunities *pl*	wirtschaftliche Möglichkeiten
educated	gebildet
empire	Imperium
Enlightenment	Aufklärung
epic poem	Heldengedicht
equivalent	Entsprechung
established	anerkannt, akzeptiert
European Economic Community	Europäische Wirtschaftsgemeinschaft

F

fair	Ausstellung, Jahrmarkt
fellow countrymen *pl*	Landsleute
fiction	Belletristik
"first past the post" system	Mehrheitswahlsystem
fortress	Festung
freshwater lake	Süßwassersee
from abroad	aus dem Ausland

G

general election	Unterhauswahlen
gherkin	Gewürzgurke
Good Friday	Karfreitag
greyhound	Windhund
grim	*hier:* hart, trostlos
growth	Wachstum
Gulf Stream	Golfstrom
gunpowder	Schießpulver
gurning	Grimassenschneiden

H

haggis	Gericht aus Schafsinnereien
Head of State	Staatsoberhaupt
heir	Erbe, Erbin
heir to the throne	Erbprinz, Erbprinzessin
Hogmanay *Scottish*	Silvester
home-brewed	hausgebraut
hospitality	Gastfreundlichkeit
to host	ausrichten, Gastgeber sein
hotpot	Eintopf
hurling	irisches Hockey

I

impressive	beeindruckend
in circulation	im Umlauf
independence	Unabhängigkeit
independent	unabhängig
influence	Einfluss
inhabitant	Einwohner(in)
inhabited	bewohnt
injured	verletzt
instalment	*hier:* Fortsetzung
invader	Eindringling
to invent	erfinden
inverted snobbery	umgekehrter Snobismus
issue	Thema

J

to join	sich anschließen, Mitglied werden
to judge	beurteilen

K

to keep oneself to oneself	für sich bleiben
kickabout	Kicken
kilt	Schottenrock
kitchen fitter	Kücheneinrichter(in)

L

lady-in-waiting	Kammerfrau
landmark	Wahrzeichen
landscaped garden	Landschaftsgarten
landslide victory	Erdrutschsieg
late	*hier:* verstorben
law	Gesetz
law of the land	geltendes Recht
liar	Lügner(in)
liner	Passagierschiff

M

male voice choir	Männerchor
medal count	Medaillenspiegel
Member of Parliament (MP)	Abgeordnete(r)

Merry England	gutes altes England
⚡ milk snatcher	Milchdieb(in)
mine	Bergwerk
miners' strike	Bergarbeiterstreik
mining	Bergbau
mint	Münzanstalt
mistress	Geliebte
monastery	Kloster
mud	Schlamm
mural	Wandgemälde
murder mystery	Krimi
mushy peas *pl*	Erbsenpüree

N

national assembly	Nationalversammlung
native speaker	Muttersprachler(in)
Neolithic	jungsteinzeitlich
9/11	der 11. September
noble	Adlige(r)
north–south divide	Nord-Süd-Gefälle
novelist	Romanautor(in)

O

observation wheel	Riesenrad
⚡ old banger	Klapperkiste
old-fashioned	altmodisch
outstanding	hervorragend

P

palm tree	Palme
pasty	Pastete, Teigtasche
patron saint	Schutzheilige(r)
penal colony	Strafkolonie
performance	Aufführung
pickled	eingelegt
to place a bet	eine Wette abgeben
plague	Pest
play	*hier:* Theaterstück
playwright	Dramatiker(in)
plinth	Sockel
plot	Verschwörung
to populate	bevölkern
population	Bevölkerung
⚡ posh	*hier:* zur Oberschicht gehörend, „schnieke"
previously	zuvor
privacy	Privatsphäre
private	*hier:* zurückhaltend, reserviert
to promote	fördern
prosperity	Wohlstand
proud	stolz
⚡ pub grub	Kneipenessen
public services *pl*	öffentliche Dienstleitungen
pun	Wortspiel
to push the boundaries	die Grenzen ausloten

Q

queue jumping	Vordrängeln

R

raid	Angriff, Überfall
raven	Rabe
regularly	regelmäßig
reign	Regentschaft
resident	Einwohner(in)
resilient	zäh, unverwüstlich
recipient	Empfänger(in)
rivalry	Rivalität
rogue	Schlingel
Royal Navy	Königliche Marine
to rule	herrschen
rural	ländlich

S

saucy	keck
savoury	herzhaft, salzig
scientific research	wissenschaftliche Forschung
self-deprecation	Selbstironie
to set the stage	die Voraussetzungen schaffen
shamrock	Kleeblatt
shard	Scherbe
shin-kicking	Schienbeintreten
shortage of workers	Arbeitskräftemangel
silk	Seide
silliness	Albernheit
single currency	Einheitswährung
skull	Schädel
slice	*hier:* Ausschnitt
sociable	gesellig, freundlich

social make-up	soziale Struktur
society	Gesellschaft
sovereignty	Souveränität
space	Raum
spices *pl*	Gewürze
splendid	prächtig
spoof	Parodie
spy	Spion(in)
square kilometre	Quadratkilometer
steamship	Dampfer
stereotype	Klischee, Vorurteil
stiff upper lip	unerschütterliche Haltung, *wörtl.* steife Oberlippe
successful	erfolgreich
superb	hervorragend
to support	unterstützen
Supreme Governor	*hier:* Kirchenoberhaupt
sword	Schwert

T

tapestry	Wandteppich
tartare sauce	Remouladensoße
to tease	necken
tensions *pl*	Spannungen
the..., the...	je ..., desto ...
thistle	Distel
to this day	bis heute
↯ toff	feiner Pinkel
to torture	foltern
tossing the caber	Baumstammwerfen
tournament	Turnier
trace	Spur
track	*hier:* Rennbahn
trade	Handel
trade union	Gewerkschaft
traitor	Verräter(in)
tribe	Volksstamm
to tut disapprovingly	missbilligend schnalzen

U

unforgivable	unverzeihlich
unique	einzigartig
united	vereinigt, vereint
uprising	Aufstand

V

vast majority	überwältigende Mehrheit
virgin	Jungfrau
vote	Stimme; Abstimmung

W

walkabout	*hier:* Bad in der Menge
wave	Welle
weight	Gewicht
witty	geistreich, witzig
World Heritage Site	Welterbestätte

Y

Yeomen Warders *pl*	königliche Leibgardisten